I USED
TO BE A
MISERABLE
F✲CK

I USED TO BE A MISERABLE F✳CK

An Everyman's Guide to a
MEANINGFUL LIFE

John Kim

First Published in the USA in 2019 by *HarperOne*, an imprint of
HarperCollins Publishers, New York, New York USA

Published in the UK in 2019 by *Short Books*,
Unit 316, ScreenWorks, 22 Highbury Grove, London N5 2ER

Published by arrangement with *HarperOne*, an imprint of
HarperCollins Publishers, New York, New York USA

10 9 8 7 6 5 4 3 2 1

A CIP catalogue record for this book is
available from the British Library.

ISBN: 978-1-78072-396-9

Cover design by Two Associates
Page layouts for this edition based on the orignal layouts for
the US edition designed by Janet M. Evans-Scanlon

Printed at CPI Group (UK) Ltd, Croydon, CR0 4YY

This book is dedicated to anyone who has been in a dark place. Who has felt lost or disconnected. Cursed their birth. Survived a shattered heart, held shitty jobs, gone through toxic relationships, and wrestled with uncertainty. Anyone who has felt grayed out and purposeless. Ugly, washed-up, wishing there was more, better, or different. This book is dedicated to anyone who has ever felt like a miserable f*ck.

Resist nothing.

CONTENTS

The ultimate measure of a man is not where he stands in moments of comfort and convenience, but where he stands at times of challenge and controversy.

– MARTIN LUTHER KING JR

The problem is, God gave man a brain and a penis and only enough blood to run one at a time.

– ROBIN WILLIAMS

Dear Men,

When I was going through my divorce, I picked up a book. It was a book about men titled *The Way of the Superior Man*, by David Deida. I'd never read a book about men before. I didn't even know books about men existed or what to expect from reading one. That book ended up changing my life. It was the first domino to fall in the long Hero's Journey that followed. That journey changed the way I thought, ate, loved, and moved. It challenged my thinking, my definitions, and my beliefs about myself. It gave me new lenses, a sense of purpose, and it repositioned me with fire in my belly to help other men on their path.

During this process, my definitions about manhood changed. I learned that they had been distorted by parents, society, advertising, and locker rooms. They were damaging. Kept me in a tight box, turning me into a cardboard cutout instead of a real growing and evolving man. I was a walking *should*, living other people's definitions instead of my own. So I cleared the slate and started over, leaned into the new, the unknown; I slayed some dragons, bought a motorcycle, got some tattoos, and grew some real balls. Not the kind that action movies are made of. But the kind that remind you that they are uneven, because you are human. I came back to the village a different person. No longer a poster. But a real person with new definitions and a mirror to check more than my hair.

My intent in writing this book isn't to put my definitions on you. It's to create a dialogue and challenge your own beliefs about what it looks like to be a man. My hope is that it encourages you to think about who you are now and who you want to be, and gives you the motivation to close that gap. I'm not here to lecture you. I'm coming *with* you, not *at* you. Talking to you like one of my friends—the men I sweat with, eat with, ride motorcycles with, get crepes and share my fucking feelings with. Yes, real men eat crepes.

You may have seen from my bio that I am a therapist. That's true. But I am not coming at you here just as a therapist. I am doing this *with* you, as a brother. As a fellow human. And although we may sometimes talk about women and relationships, this isn't about Mars or Venus. About us versus them. This is about being a better version of yourself. Plain and simple. It's about connection. Discovery. Building. It's about evolving, expanding, and living closer to your truth and potential. Not only for you, but for all of us.

Because the world desperately needs present fathers, loyal brothers, loving boyfriends, strong husbands, vulnerable leaders, and sharp men to sharpen other men.

We need to take back ownership of the role that men play in our world.

It's time for our return.

– John Kim, the Angry Therapist

Introduction

Boys get their definitions of manhood, strength, love, and self from watching other men—specifically, their dads. But we live in a fatherless nation. I learned this firsthand when I was working as a therapist at a nonprofit, treating teenagers for addiction. After working with hundreds of teens and their parents, I realized that the common thread in over 95 percent of these troubled teens was an absent father. Dad was either physically or emotionally gone. The girls stood too close to me, desperate for "Dad's" attention, and, without anyone to teach them boundaries, were easily confused in social interactions with authority figures. But after my weeks of working with them, they quickly picked up on social cues and acceptable ways to communicate.

The boys were another story. Many of them mimicked everything I did, following me around, looking for an example of how to do the most mundane, obvious things. A few of them were confrontational, hoping for a connection with another man but never taught how to receive male affection or attention without posturing, panicking, and showing physical aggression. Both behaviors, I realized, stem from not having a positive, healthy male role model at home, and both behaviors can follow middle-schoolers into high school, then college, then the workplace, and into relationships with family members, colleagues, and loved ones for the rest of their lives. Unlike the girls, the boys didn't learn quickly. They were, truthfully, lost.

The boys I worked with were growing up stunted, with a warped definition of "man". Throw in manipulative advertising, toxic locker rooms, and today's scroll-and-swipe culture that promotes instant gratification and hiding, and it's no surprise that many of these boys go on to define themselves by having muscles or a corner office, learning about love, sex, and intimacy through dating apps and pornography. For many boys, intimacy is only skin-deep, and courting a potential partner is something they do while sitting on the toilet on their phone, where they never learn to communicate or experience true connection. Ultimately, their relationships fail, and because they don't know what healthy feels like or have no tools to fix what's broken, they fall into unhealthy relationship loops that prevent learning and growth. Such a boy has now created his own prison. Perhaps he forms unhealthy beliefs about himself, women, and love. *I'm not good enough. I'm not lovable.* This may lead to anger and coping strategies like addictions, ghosting, and passionless communication—things that only disconnect him from his self. He may feel debilitating shame or guilt, and he may even lash out at his partner, his family, or perfect strangers. He becomes a predator. Now suddenly he experiences isolation, depression, and more false beliefs, which are fueled by more flawed and ineffective reactions. Women now become objects. Or, more accurately, prey.

Regardless of the specific road that leads him there, all paths like the one above lead to the same place: men everywhere feeling lost or misunderstood, living without purpose and passion, and needing to inflate physical or superficial details to make up for what's lacking on the inside. Or giving up altogether.

And all of this impacts us directly. In the US alone, according to the American Foundation for Suicide Prevention, forty-five thousand people commit suicide each year. Out of those, 79 percent are men. While women are more prone to having suicidal thoughts, men are more likely to actually do it. Some six million men in America are diagnosed with depression annually. While depressed women are more likely to report feelings of sadness, helplessness, and guilt, men are more likely to suffer in silence and not seek treatment. Researchers say it is often more difficult for men to identify their illness. Men with depression are more likely to report fatigue, irritability, and loss of interest in work. You probably don't need me to tell you that 99 percent of mass shootings are reportedly done by men.

I can't talk about men without talking about women, who for far too long have suffered at the hands of boys who fail to grow up into men. As reported by the Huffington Post, 85 percent of all victims of domestic violence are women. One in three women has been a victim of some form of physical violence by an intimate partner within her lifetime. Domestic violence is the third leading cause of homelessness among families, with 50 percent of all women who are homeless reporting that domestic violence was the immediate cause of their leaving home, according to the National Center on Family Homelessness. And of course this trickles down to the children. According to the World Health Organization, some 40 to 60 percent of men who abuse women also abuse children. One out of every five teenage girls says she has been in a relationship where the boyfriend threatened violence or self-harm if a breakup were to occur.

Finally women are feeling safe enough to come forward and share their stories in the world, and what this has revealed more than ever is that the root of the problems facing women is . . . well, men. I'm not saying women are perfect, but they are not the ones assaulting, raping, and physically abusing other people. That said, I understand that many men are emotionally abused by women. All of this abuse feeds on itself, and the cycle needs to be broken. It's not about blame; it's about taking responsibility. And since I am a man, I am talking to and focusing on men. Now more than ever, we have a duty to take ownership and redefine ourselves. And women must raise the bar and set a standard for the kind of men they want in their lives.

Okay, but how? After all, we are not born men. We are born boys. Although we may take the shape of a man on the exterior, the transition into manhood is an internal process. One that requires much work: reflection, pain, courage, and sometimes a rebirth. It is a process that never ends. There is no completion. Being a man is a journey. Many choose to embark on this journey. Many do not. If you do not, you will never develop, evolve, and become the best version of yourself. Manhood is not a light switch. It is not about age. You don't become a man just because you turn eighteen. Being a man is a way of life; it's about everyday choices that lead you to live toward your potential. If you choose not to embark on this journey, your relationships with friends and family, your work life, and your ability to create authentic intimacy will never be realized. I know. I was a boy most of my life. And as the title of this book suggests, I used to be a miserable fuck.

I grew up in the '80s. I was raised by television, magazines, and anything/everything pop culture because my parents were never home. They were working eighteen-hour days to live the "American Dream". I had complete freedom. I did what I wanted. I ate what I wanted. I watched what I wanted.

Even though I was alone most of the time, I never blamed my parents. I knew they were doing the best they could. They never learned about emotional intelligence, about how to communicate in a healthy way and create safe spaces. Because of this, I never talked about my feelings, and I never learned how to manage my energy and my emotions. This meant I entered adulthood without tools. I was highly reactive, controlling, and irresponsible, and I had little self-awareness. Of course, this rolled into all my relationships and created beautiful dysfunction.

Before I talk about my divorce, I want to mention that I made a promise to myself to share only my side of this story, without using names. I am very protective of my ex-wife and her anonymity. Although she is not in my life anymore, she is an exceptional human being, and I have nothing but love and respect for her and her family. They are beautiful people who have significantly contributed to my "man journey". I also believe, as a man, that we should protect the people we have loved, no matter what happened. I believe we grow through all our collisions.

In any case, I knew I was going to marry her when she first walked into our family restaurant. After twenty years of slaving in fast food, my parents finally saved up enough money to buy a nice little eatery—and by "nice" I mean something I wasn't embarrassed about—that catered to the production studios in Hollywood. I was in my twenties and running the place because, well, my parents barely spoke English and had no idea what the hell they were doing. The truth is, neither did I. Anyway, she was nineteen and had just come to Los Angeles from Oregon. She didn't have any plans to stay. She was actually looking for a job for a friend. She had no experience in the restaurant business, and we didn't need any more servers. But I hired her because she made my heart stop. It was like a scene in a movie. I literally heard angels. We quickly became friends, and one night, after a private party and a few drinks, I kissed her in the office—an Airstream trailer in the back patio. I knew that if she didn't kiss me back I could blame it on the alcohol, since it takes me only one beer to get drunk. (That's why they called me "glow worm" in college.) But surprisingly, she kissed me back. And the rest of our story zooms by like a montage in a romance film, before the turbulence. Quick shots of us—two kids in Hollywood exploring young love. She was acting. I was screenwriting. There was something romantic about two kids pursuing their dreams in Tinseltown. Running a restaurant that later became a trendy supper club. Me leaving brown-bag lunches with little notes on them on her porch. Swimming naked in my parents' pool like two kids ditching school. We fell, deep and fast.

I asked her to marry me on a mountaintop in Oregon. I dropped to one knee and believed we would be together forever. We exchanged our own written vows, and I cried in front of a hundred people. I remember a dude making fun of me for my love tears. I was embarrassed, because real men don't cry at their wedding. We moved in together—and then a sobering reality hit. Our movie switched genres, from a romance film to a gritty documentary. It became very clear I wasn't raised with any tools. She had missed the fine print. I never made my bed. I peed in the shower. I left little hairs in the sink after shaving. (Every woman reading this just got it.) I didn't clean up after myself. I ate out more than we could afford. And I lived in coffee shops, trying to write the million-dollar screenplay so I could be a "real man" and we could "live the dream". But of course that never happened. So I became unhappy. Insecure. Lost. Negative. Jealous. Controlling. And miserable.

In a nutshell, I went from her mouth to her nipple, from her man to her son. I went from a twenty-something-year-old running a scenic restaurant bar in Hollywood with tons of friends and fresh ambition to an insecure screenwriter who never made his bed and asked permission to buy sugar cereal. Of course, the dynamic changed. And instead of taking responsibility, I blamed her and the marriage. It wasn't until I went through the ensuing divorce and the rebirth that happened after it that I began to look at my own defects and question who I was, who I wanted to be, and my definition of what a man looks like. I started by looking inward. I started to observe the way I thought and behaved, and why. I examined my cognitive distortions, false beliefs, and flawed wiring. I took responsibility for my actions. I learned how they impact not only others but also my path. I became aware of my state and how that rippled through my everyday quality of life and productivity. I learned about love and the importance of self-love. I discovered the power of vulnerability. I learned about forgiveness. I learned about feminine and masculine energy. All this changed me, my relationships, and, of course, my life.

Simply put, I became a man.

The following is a collection of behavioral traits that helped me on my path, dos and don'ts that point you down the road to becoming an authentic man. No one has time for dense theories that don't make sense in everyday life. So I put descriptions of each of these traits into a shot glass for you, simple and easy to digest. These are based on thousands of sessions I've done as a licensed therapist with both men and women, studying relationship patterns. But also, and more important, they are based on my own journey crossing that great divide from boy to man. Slaying my own dragons, and coming back to the village with revelations to share.

I still struggle with many of the traits I discuss in this book. Being a man is not about perfection or completion. It's a process, a journey. But once you embark on your journey, you will realize there are foundational traits that define your character and position you for greater things. You may or may not agree with me as to the importance of these traits. Some are light. Some are heavy. But I believe they contribute to healthier relationships in all forms—especially your relationship with yourself—and make you a better man.

SELF

Welcome to Part One. We're not starting with your fucked-up love life or frustrations with dating, your lopsided friendships, or the tyre around your waist you just can't get rid of. We're not starting with your controlling parents who still have a power over you that you will not admit to, or the micromanaging partners of your new startup that's going to make you billions. We are starting with your *self*. Why? Because every journey begins and ends with you.

The self is relating to a system of social, psychological, neural, and molecular mechanisms—a bundle of perceptions, an immortal soul that transcends the physical. Basically, it's an abstract word in psychology that wellness today has loaded with excuses. Yes, there is your core, your soul, your spirit, the essence of who you are; and loving and feeding those parts is important. But that is not enough. The self is a fancy word for answering the question, *Who are you?* And the answer is created through action.

THE SELF,
in a shot glass:

Men are vulnerable. Men are aware of their thoughts and actions. Men don't react, they respond. Men realize that freedom is not the opposite of responsibility. Men let the world work through them, not at them. Men are humble. Men don't bully, whine, or judge. Men are compassionate. Men are kind. Men create their own happiness.

#1
Don't Hide

I remember the first time I saw a man really be vulnerable. I was married at the time. My father-in-law was driving me and my then wife, his daughter, to the airport. She had been telling a story in the truck about how difficult high school had been. After hearing the story, my father-in-law started to cry. He had no idea she had been bullied. He thought she had had a great high school experience. I remember seeing the tears stream down his face, the hurt and empathy in his eyes. But more importantly, he saw how that made my wife at the time feel. Because he wasn't always like that. He had raised her with an iron fist and kept his emotions buried. It wasn't until he went through his own divorce that he started to really show himself and express his feelings. I remember watching this like a scene out of a father/daughter movie and thinking, *Wow, he's not afraid to show himself, not only to his daughter, but also to me.* Just hours before, he and I had been lifting weights and talking about motorcycles.

And yet there he was, sobbing because he was feeling his daughter's pain. He apologized for not being present when she was going through high school. He apologized for not being there for her. He apologized for being an absent father. Then she started to cry. Then I started to cry. We were all crying inside this truck as we headed to the airport. And in that moment, my definition of what a real man looks like changed.

There's something about the word "vulnerability" that

repels men. And yet most of us can admit that vulnerability is a good thing, that it often leads to success, that it can give you strength. But there's a difference between watching and agreeing with the science-backed power of vulnerability on a TED talk and actually practicing it in real life. We keep vulnerability at arm's length. We nod our heads. We agree. But we don't execute. We don't deploy. We hide.

Webster's defines "vulnerable" as "capable of or susceptible to being wounded or hurt." And that's exactly how most men see it. Which is why we hold up our shield. We don't show ourselves through vulnerability and instead try to show ourselves in other ways: by fixing things, by paying our bills on time, by being the loudest one in the room.

This conditioning runs deep. It's been passed down from our fathers and grandfathers who demonstrated that feelings are meant to be kept inside, and from locker rooms and fraternity houses where we were taught to "man the fuck up".

As we enter adulthood, there is only more and more reason to hide our true selves. We get hurt. Our hearts harden. Talking about feelings is something women do. We're men.

But vulnerability isn't just about talking about your feelings. It's about showing your true self. For many of us, we don't show ourselves until we have to. Until there's something at stake. Until we lose something—a relationship, a marriage, a friendship, a business, and eventually ourselves. We get to a place where we have nowhere else to go. But until then, we bottle things up. And we cope by letting that shit come out in unhealthy ways. We develop and then feed addictions, become workaholics; we may even cheat, lie, get aggressive, or let ourselves be doormats.

But more importantly, if we don't show our true selves and express how we feel, we are denying ourselves. We are telling ourselves we don't matter. We are turning ourselves invisible.

Practicing vulnerability isn't about doing something for others. You're not doing someone a favor. You're not giving in. You're creating soil, rich soil, for you and your growth. You're raising your potential. You're positioning yourself. You're building a better, stronger you. Everything starts with your truth. Nothing can be built without it.

In doing thousands of sessions with couples for the last decade, I've found the biggest complaint from women is that their partner is not vulnerable, not communicating, not showing himself and expressing his feelings. I want you to think about this. If I talked to your girlfriend/wife/partner/female colleague/lady friend, would she have the same thing to say about you? Be honest with yourself.

Everything starts with your truth.
Nothing can be built without it.

Not showing vulnerability, not being transparent with the people in your life, creates a disconnect. You're leaving the other person in the dark. You're doing life *around* your partner instead of *with* your partner. He or she feels alone. You're taking a crowbar to your relationship instead of producing glue, and you won't be able to build anything healthy and sustaining.

So ask yourself, *Am I being vulnerable? Am I showing myself?* Not just with your partner. In all your relationships. With friends. Coworkers. Employees. Your boss. Your children. Parents. Family. If not, why? Are you still holding on to old definitions of what a man looks like? If so, maybe it's time to change your definitions. Because here's the truth: if you don't practice vulnerability, you will never reach your full potential as a father, brother, boyfriend, husband, friend, son, teacher, leader, entrepreneur, and human.

2
Do Walk with Mirrors

For most of my life, the only thing I did with a mirror was check my hair. I thought self-awareness was skin-deep.

When I was married, I thought I was a very self-aware person. I expressed myself and my feelings often, more than the average John. I was sensitive and thoughtful and was praised for it. I was the guy in my circle of friends everyone came to for advice. I was very aware of what I was good at and not good at. I wasn't academic but I was creative. I wasn't organized but I was prolific. I knew myself. But that's only self-awareness on the surface.

I also steamrolled people, tried to get them to understand me without trying to understand them, always pulled from logic, and found many faults in others but rarely in myself. That's because I never looked inward. Self-awareness means looking inward and being aware of how your thoughts, actions, and energy impact others. Doing this not just once, but all the time. It's not just about knowing yourself. It's what you decide to do with that knowing. That's self-awareness.

I eventually realized, through many expired relationships, that maybe the problem or part of the problem was me. This opened up a whole new world, a hard world to face. It was a revelation. I was living in a bubble, oblivious to the damage I was doing. Not only to others but to myself.

If vulnerability is soil, self-awareness is the seeds we plant for growth. Everything starts with self-awareness. We all have a veneer, an outside shell that has been formed by society, advertising, parents, and old blueprints, and we use this shell to protect ourselves. We craft a version of ourselves to present to the world, and it often causes us to seek approval and validation instead of looking inward, examining our thoughts, our behaviors, and our effect on others.

In order to build self-awareness, we must be metacognitive—that is, have active control over our cognitive processes, think about our thinking, know about our knowing, be aware of our awareness, and explore our wiring and make a motion to rewire. It's this type of higher thinking that separates children from adults, boys from men.

To walk with mirrors is a daily self-examination. Growth and truth are not destinations. They are states. You have to put yourself in those states for truth and growth to happen. And the only way to get into those states is to always look inward. Until it becomes a way of life.

How to walk with mirrors

Here are my top three tips for learning to walk with mirrors and thereby become more self-aware.

1. MEDITATE.

I'll be honest with you: like many, I struggle with meditation. But only if you define meditation as sitting cross-legged on the floor with my palms facing up, eyes closed, and listening to an app. Meditation can come in many forms. It's the daily practice of creating distance between you and your thoughts by focusing on your breath and anchoring yourself using your senses. Because most of our thoughts are distortions, and those distortions pull us out of the here and now and into time machines. We live in the future or past and become walking reactions. How you meditate (i.e., practice creating this distance) is up to you. I meditate by riding my motorcycle. I mediate on walks. I meditate during my fitness workouts. What matters is that you do it and do it often.

2. LOOK AT WHAT'S COMING UP.

As we interact with people throughout our day, shit comes up. People trigger us. This is because of our stories and wiring. There are dynamics in our relationships that make us angry or resistant or avoidant. People remind us of other people who have hurt us, loved us, and raised us. Practicing self-awareness means looking at what comes up when we engage with these people—objectively, from a bird's-eye point of view. And then separating what's theirs to own and what's ours.

3. OWN YOUR SHIT. (SEE P.131.)

Now you take responsibility by doing something about it. This may mean practicing nonjudgment. Compassion. Forgiveness. But it always means responding instead of reacting. And that requires a beat. A pause. Some thought. Self-reflection. It means being aware of how your energy and actions affect others, and taking responsibility for them. Create distance from your thoughts so that you are not living your cognitive distortions, so that you're looking at what's coming up (your feelings) when you engage with people who trigger you or bring out your resistance, owning your own shit by knowing what is yours, and taking responsibility by choosing to respond responsibly. Not just once, but every . . . single . . . day. That's what self-awareness looks like. Of course there will be easier days and harder days. But the choice to practice self-awareness daily is walking with mirrors.

If you don't walk with mirrors, you'll never establish anything real. You become a walking shell. But after you begin to look inward, you'll start to become curious about yourself, how you think, why you think the way you do. Your conscious choice to be aware of how your thoughts and actions affect not only your life but the lives of others, and to do something about it, is what will position you to become more. Any man can build abs. Any man can make money. But men who walk with mirrors are true leaders.

3
Do Choose Responsibility over Freedom

I was working out with my friend Justin this morning. Justin is the father of two daughters. He also loves working out. He claims that no matter how shit-faced he has gotten the night before or how much sleep he didn't get or what life has thrown at him, he never misses a workout. For him, working out is freedom from his responsibilities. He always gets that in.

A while back, we were only a quarter of the way done with his favorite workout when he told me he had to leave. Surprised, I asked him where he was going. He said he had to go pick up his daughter. But not in a "Shit, I gotta go," complaining way. It was very matter-of-fact. It was a choice. A decision that was made. A line was drawn, with no looking back.

I understand it's just a workout, but if you know Justin like I know Justin, that workout is everything. Nevertheless, he chose responsibility over freedom. There was no hesitation. He could have called his wife or paid the babysitter to stay longer. However, in his mind, picking up his daughter was his duty. It was important to him that *he* do it and that he not show up late.

I think about this moment with Justin often. I think about it because when I put myself in Justin's position, I find myself wondering if I would have done the same thing. I might have figured out a way to finish my "freedom". I would have convinced myself that it's not a big deal. *I pick up my daughter every day. She can wait ten minutes.* But it's not about the ten minutes. It's about your definition of a man. Or in this case, a father. By Justin's actions, we know very well what his definition of a father is. It's clear-cut, black-and-white: responsibility over freedom.

I've always thought that freedom was a right. That it's given. Fuck, I live in America! The land of the free. Right? Maybe. But when it comes to being a man, freedom is not given. It is earned, by being responsible. You choose to be responsible first. You show up to work when you don't feel like it. You put in the hours when you're tired. You plan date night when you don't feel romantic. You call your parents because they matter. You express how you feel even though you don't want to. You practice self-care even though it's hard because you're not used to it. Through the action of being responsible, trust is built. When you have trust, you have freedom. You have earned it. But if you always choose freedom over responsibility, you will be breaking trust. Not only with others but with yourself. You won't trust that you can build anything, whether it be an empire or a marriage. You will be doing only what feels good and easy in the moment, and that is my definition of a boy. Not a man. Of course, all of this hangs on my definition of man. It may not be yours. But that is why our definitions are so important. They shape us.

Justin's story is one simple example of what responsibility can look like.

What does responsibility look like for you?

Personally, I have a responsibility to create a dialogue every single day. It doesn't matter on what platform: through my blog, a Facebook LIVE stream, my podcast, or maybe in person. Since I got my first follower on Tumblr nearly a decade ago, I have felt pulled to create content. I believe I

Definitions matter.

Definitions are your starting line. You cannot make the jump from boy to man without defining things for yourself and taking pride in your definitions. It isn't about adopting my definitions, though; it's about creating your own. Throughout this book I'll ask you to define words for yourself: "vulnerability", "compassion", "douche", etc. Creating clear definitions will allow you to better understand whether you are being the version of yourself that you want to be, or whether you are falling short of your expectations.

have a responsibility to help others through my writing. It lines up with my story and everything I went through. I also have a responsibility to stand on my truth and live by example in my "real" life, which includes the dos and don'ts in this book.

I fall short, often. But I have a responsibility to be honest with myself. I have a responsibility to work on myself. I have a responsibility to practice transparency, compassion, and gratitude, to try to be the best human I can, given where I'm at. I make those my responsibilities because they matter to me. They are what make me me. They are what make me a man, according to my definition. Without them, my life doesn't have meaning. I lose my legs.

So ask yourself, *What is my responsibility today? Am I choosing freedom instead?* If you prioritized your responsibilities, would there be freedom in there as well? What might that freedom look like or feel like?

#4
Do Live a
Through-Me Life

I lived most of my life with a "to-me" mind-set. Something happened *to* me. She dumped me. He took something *from* me. Life did something *to* me. Or nothing happened *to* me. When something happens *to* you, you're in victim mode—the most powerless state.

Yes, things happen in our lives that we have no control over. We get bullied. We get into car accidents. People we love die unexpectedly. But we have a choice in what kind of mind-set to have, what lenses to see the world through. If we believe that everything happens *to* us, as I did, we lose our power. We walk through life with hunched shoulders, just waiting for the next thing to happen or not happen to us. We create our own prison by living what I call a to-me life. Children—or in this case, boys—live in this state. Someone steals their toy and they instantly see themselves as victims. They cry and pout and throw peas at the wall. But they're allowed to. Because they don't have the tools and awareness to understand anything else. Many grown men do their version of this. Something happens in life that they don't like or expect—they lose their job, the promotion, the race, the girl—and they instantly become victims. They complain. They blame. And they let everyone around them know how unhappy they are.

What was your reaction the last time someone broke up with you? Did you assassinate her character? Talk shit about her to your friends? Demand that she return the couch you

Fixed mind-set versus growth mind-set.

Carol Dweck, one of the leading researchers in the field of motivation, did a study at Stanford University on what made people successful and unsuccessful. She discovered that the greatest difference between people who are successful and people who are not successful is their mind-set. Successful people have a growth mind-set. Unsuccessful people have a fixed mind-set.

The thinking and behavior produced by living a to-me life is a fixed mind-set. The thinking and behavior produced by living a through-me life is a growth mind-set.

bought her? What about when the server messed up your dinner order? When someone cut you off on the road? Took your parking space? What did you do? Flip them off? Curse them out? Yes, that comes from anger. More accurately, from not being able to control your anger. But that anger comes from feeling like a victim. Someone did something to you. Took something from you. A relationship? A parking spot? Time? Love? Self-worth?

On the other end of the spectrum is what I call the through-me mind-set. This is where there is very little ego. Because it's not about you. You are a conduit, and something greater than you is working *through you* to project your unique gifts into the world. This is the most power-filled state. Because in order to be in this state you must believe in something bigger than yourself. It's not about you. And when you don't make it about you, you are powerful.

Ego shrinks us. When you're living a through-me life, without all of that ego to blind you and weigh you down, you become fearless. When someone dumps you, you accept it and move on. Yes, you may feel pain and maybe some anger. But you accept and own that pain and that anger and ultimately wish the best for the other person. When someone cuts you off, you feel sorry for or empathy with the other person. There is more room for compassion and forgiveness. No one is taking anything from you. You have control. You are power-filled.

You are a conduit, and something greater than you is working *through you* to project your unique gifts into the world.

If you want to do big things in the world, to make any kind of dent in the universe, you must live a through-me life.

Mind-sets, in a shot glass:

Fixed mind-set (to-me): I'm either good or I'm not. When I'm frustrated, I give up. I don't like to be challenged. When I fail, I'm no good. Tell me that I'm smart. If you succeed, I feel threatened. My abilities determine everything.

Growth mind-set (through-me): I can learn anything I want to. When I'm frustrated, I persevere. I want to challenge myself. When I fail, I learn. Tell me that I try hard. If you succeed, I'm inspired. My efforts and attitude determine everything.

#5
Don't Be
a Double Douche

Okay, the truth is that every man was or will be a douche at some point in his life.

Here are some examples of douche behavior: Purchasing a bright yellow Ferrari because you can, not because you're a car enthusiast but because you like making a big scene wherever you roll up. Being a dick to the elderly or children. Checking yourself in every reflection. Offensive tattoos meant for attention. Super-crunchy hair. Not controlling your alcohol intake. Groping women. Starting fights with men because you know some form of martial arts. Fake bake. Teeth that glow in the dark. Sporting sunglasses indoors. Controlling your partner. Being the loudest voice in the room, on purpose. Flavored condoms. Animal cruelty. Pulling in front of the car that cut you off and slamming on your brakes. Not tipping. Tossing your keys at the valet guy instead of just handing them to him. Way too much cologne. Demanding to speak to the restaurant manager in front of your company. V-necks that meet at your belly button. Refusing to turn down your car stereo while people are trying to have a conversation. Being creepy. Riding motorcycles that set off car alarms. Bullying. Cursing and using graphic sexual language in front of women. Overtipping to impress others. Ghosting. Asking people you don't know well how much money they make. Telling people you don't know how much money *you* make. Screaming like you're giving birth while you're working out. Walking across the street when everyone else is waiting for the Walk light except you. Road rage. Driving recklessly. Going halves on the check on the first date when you asked him or her out. Talking over people. Being an asshole to your parents. Belching in public. Putting people down. Talking shit about others. Name-dropping. Asking your partner about her sexual history because you're "just curious", then judging her for it. Treating your employees like shit. Using your job position to sexually harass.

Those are just a few examples, and I'm 100 percent positive I've got punched holes on my douche card.

Although it may feel empowering, this behavior does nothing but announce our insecurity. And everyone knows it. They talk about us. Word spreads. When I play back my life, my douchery was the most prevalent when I felt the most insecure. *Being a douche is like turning on a black light that exposes your insecurities.* For me, it was my club daze (. . . exactly). My family-owned restaurant bar in Hollywood. I partnered with a club promoter to turn it into a scenic supper club for the rich and famous. It lasted only about a year, but it was one crazy year. Back in 2001, when hip-hop was at its peak and the club scene in Hollywood was bubbling, Paris Hilton, Fred Durst, and a bunch of other celebrities used our little family business as the quad. Being surrounded by shiny people and things tugged on every insecurity I had. I felt I was a part of the "cool kids", but I didn't feel like I belonged. I wasn't rich or famous. I was the kid from the other side of the tracks. And in order to fit in, I had to prove that I did. I would ignore people yelling my name at the door. I would walk like I mattered, even though I didn't believe I did. I would comp six-hundred-dollar dinners in exchange for approval. I would purposely sit at tables draped with "beautiful" people even though I didn't know any of them personally. I would posture every night, and it was fucking exhausting. I wasn't building character. I was creating a caricature.

Douchebaggery

Robert Moore and Douglas Gillette describe douchebaggery beautifully in their book *King, Warrior, Magician, Lover: Rediscovering the Archetypes of the Mature Masculine*:

> The drug dealer, the ducking and diving political leader, the wife beater, the chronically "crabby" boss, the "hot shot" junior executive, the unfaithful husband, the company "yes man," the indifferent graduate school adviser, the "holier than thou" minister, the gang member, the father who can never find the time to attend his daughter's school programs, the coach who ridicules his star athletes, the therapist who unconsciously attacks his clients' "shining" and seeks a kind of gray normalcy for them, the yuppie—all these men have something in common. They are all boys pretending to be men. They got that way honestly, because nobody showed them what a mature man is like.... We are continually mistaking this man's controlling, threatening, hostile behaviors for strength. In reality, he is showing an underlying extreme vulnerability and weakness, the vulnerability of the wounded boy.
>
> The devastating fact is that most men are fixated at an immature level of development. These early developmental levels are governed by the inner blueprints appropriate to boyhood. When they are allowed to rule what should be adulthood, when the archetypes of boyhood are not built upon and transcended by the Ego's appropriate accessing of the archetypes of mature masculinity, they cause us to act out of our hidden (to us, but seldom to others) boyishness.

So how do you stop being a douche? Is it as simple as selling that yellow Ferrari?

1. Prove nothing

We posture because we want to prove something. What we have. Who we know. How rich, smart, and jacked we are. The intention/action of trying to announce it to the world is what makes us come off as a douche. We are tap-dancing and saying, "Look at me because I'm better than you." And that's what makes us come off as a douche: the message that we are better. Truly confident people don't need to prove anything. They focus on giving their value instead of announcing it.

Also, it's a shit ton of wasted energy. If you're always trying to prove something, you are not being your true self. Like love and hate, you can't do both at the same time. So if you're in proving mode, you are not in your authentic-self mode, which means you are maneuvering at a lower potential. You are not all that you can be.

What if you didn't feel the need to prove anything? What would that look like in your everyday life? How would that change your dialogue, behavior, attitude, and energy?

2. Be a student

When we believe we know something is when we stop learning. Deciding to be a student instantly takes us off the stage and into the classroom of life. This is where humility lives. But, more importantly, growth as well. Of course you know things. You may be an expert in your field. But if you approach everything as if you're learning it for the first time, you will be more open, curious, and likable. Judgment and ego shrink, you go from narrow to wide, and learning and becoming a better version of you become natural and effortless.

It doesn't matter if you're the CEO of a *Fortune* 500 company, a teacher, a coach, a film director. The best leaders are teachers, and teachers see themselves as students. So what would it look like to approach your day as a student? At work. With your craft. With love. How would that change your dialogue, behavior, attitude, and energy?

3. Turn your dial to give

When we call attention to ourselves, we are not giving. We are taking. We are seeking approval and validation. We want something from others. True giving means sharing you and your gifts without wanting anything back. This is when you are the most powerful.

Many times, we think we're giving when we're actually taking. For example, making a grand gesture by picking up the check and announcing "I got it" in front of the entire table is very different from discreetly paying without anyone knowing. You may think you're giving, but you're actually taking.

What would it look like to turn your dial from Take to Give? What would that look like at work? In your relationships. With your partner. What would it look like to not make it about you in your words, actions, attitude, and energy?

If you have nothing to prove, you're a student of life, and you keep your dial on Give, you don't have to sell your Ferrari.

#6
Do Starve Your Ego

Speaking of my club days, here's one of my favorite stories. As I mentioned before, I got to hang out with some celebrities. One night, I met a rapper (who I don't want to name because I don't want to gossip and be a double douche). You couldn't talk to him. Literally. You had to "go through his people". I didn't know this, and I remember walking up to him and trying to ask him what he wanted to drink or if he wanted the VIP room. And he just stood there looking straight ahead, completely ignoring me. He knew I was there and asking him a question, but he wouldn't acknowledge me. God forbid someone should see him talking to a regular person!! I remember feeling stupid. Small. I enjoyed his music, but his arrogance really turned me off. It was difficult to appreciate his music after that experience.

Then there was this other celebrity, an actor. His name was Matt Damon. The club was closed, and he sat with me and my club promoter in our VIP room (a vintage Airstream trailer) for, like, three hours. And I remember him treating us like we all went to high school together. There was no arrogance. He came back the next night and was exactly the same guy.

I share this story because, although both men were undeniably successful, I didn't see the rapper as a man. I saw him as afraid and hiding behind the shield of his own hype. He pulled from his ego instead of his heart. I'm sure Matt Damon knows he's famous. I'm sure he's used to people approaching him and wanting something. But he refused to

TOP THREE SHOTS
for killing your ego:
a daily practice

1. Smash the scoreboard

Focus less on outcomes. Instead, focus on the process. When we put all our chips on what we need to achieve, our ego is on the line. Because we tie our worth (ego) to our ability. We believe that if we don't accomplish what we set out to accomplish—close the deal, land the raise, get the girl, win the race—we are diminished, "less than". Our ego protects itself by doing everything it can to score, causing us, at times, to compromise our truth, values, and character. But by *not* focusing on the scoreboard, we stop feeding our ego. We disengage from the pissing contest. Whether it's comparisons with others or ourselves, the act of comparing strips us away from seeking the nectar in our journey, and instead we're out to prove something. Smash the scoreboard and you smash your ego.

2. Destroy your time machine

The ego does not live in the here and now. If we are fully present, there is no ego. Only truth. What *is*. Not what will be or could be or what was or could have been. There is only right now. The way you destroy your time machine is to live mindfully. Stay out of your thoughts. Stop future-tripping or dwelling on the past, all the shit you can't control. Instead use your senses to ground yourself. Breathe. Be present.

3. Pick purpose over passion

Passion is not a bad thing. It drives us. But passion can also fuel our ego. By placing purpose over passion, our ego is tamed. Anytime we make life about something greater than ourselves, we slap duct tape over our ego's mouth. If you allow your purpose, the greater good, to be your true north, you will be less concerned about your problems and fears and more concerned about the kind of dent you can make. Always hang your purpose above your passion and your ego will fall in line, be checked. Your purpose not just in your work, but also as a father, brother, husband, and friend.

buy into his projection. Instead, he showed his true self. He was *with* us instead of *at* us. He practiced a courageous amount of humility.

I say "practiced" because humility is not a button you push. It requires a daily practice. You must break down the grandiose, exaggerated idea of yourself projected by your ego. Ego leaks in slowly and is one of the most formidable things that will get in the way of your becoming a better man. Ego slowly inflates like a balloon. It happens when you get the girl. The raise. The car. The corner office. When you are given power, a microphone, a stage, a second chance. This ego balloon is actually filled with fear. Fear of not being liked. Understood. Noticed.

Practicing humility means popping this fear balloon, and starving your ego.

When you are practicing humility, you believe the world doesn't owe you dick. You are living without entitlement, and without fear. It is only you and the world, working in harmony. And the longer you stand in this space, the more present you will become, the more confidence you'll have, and the less often fear and ego will distort your sense of self.

By practicing humility, you are saying there are things you don't know. You are a student. And that's the only way you will keep learning and growing. Once you think you know, you have stopped learning. You are full. You are done. A real man is never done. He is always searching and growing. He is always a student of the world and of the people he meets, and you can't be a student without practicing humility.

The common thread in all great leaders is humility. When we are humble, we are open. There is space for self-understanding, awareness, and reflection. We have a suggestion box that brings us down from our pedestal. There is room for unity to be formed, which then builds trust. Trust allows people to feel safe. Cohesion is created, and the group, partnership, marriage, company, classroom, or nation is ready to be led, to move forward and change.

Many of us associate being perfect with being powerful and therefore think that humility equals weakness. But the truth is the complete opposite.

If we are self-centered, egotistical, or entitled, we are closed. We are cement. There is no discussion. Only pointed fingers. We sit high, looking down. This does not allow space for self-understanding or awareness. Without this space, there is no opportunity for a suggestion box. And without a suggestion box there can be no unity and no trust. People feel unsafe. There is no growth.

We all have an ego. To check that ego is difficult. It goes against our nature. It means accepting that we are not perfect. Many of us associate being perfect with being powerful and therefore think that humility equals weakness. But the truth is the complete opposite. Only when we have accepted our imperfections can we be truly powerful.

Many people mistake humility for a lack of confidence. Don't mistake the two. People who listen more than they speak, who observe first, often have the smartest things to say, display the most leadership qualities, find the most fulfillment in work and relationships, and connect people instead of driving wedges between them. Think about all the people you respect and admire in this world, and ask yourself how many of them display a sense of superiority, preach instead of teach, put themselves first, brag, talk at you instead of to you. My guess is zero. You may respect and admire someone's confidence or ability, but that does not mean you respect and admire *them*. Or that you would want to work for them or learn from them. There is a difference. Only the humble can truly lead.

#7
Don't Fuck with People Just Because You Can

Bullies aren't just angry kids on the playground. They're grown adults. They run companies, wear uniforms, and raise families. The act of bullying is not just physical. There is emotional bullying, financial bullying, spiritual bullying, mental bullying—to name a few. Ultimately, a bully is someone who tries to take away someone else's power so they feel like they have more. Most likely, it's because they were bullied as well. You've heard the saying "Hurt people hurt people"? It's true. Everyone who ever bullied me was beat up or emotionally abused by a brother, dad, uncle, or the neighborhood kids. Someone took their power away at some point in their lives, and they're trying to take that power back by taking it away from others. On a deeper level, someone took away their sense of worth, and they think that by making someone else feel small, they can feel powerful.

The first time I bullied someone was in seventh grade. I hung out with the cool kids, so no one really bullied me. You know how in every PE class, there's always one unnecessarily aggressive oversize man-child all the kids are afraid of? Well, this guy was in my class and he bullied others, but never bullied me because I was "cool". But he did always egg me on to do stupid shit. And since I was afraid of him, I usually did it. Anyway, one day when this other kid in our class and I got into a minor argument, the man-child egged me on to fight him. I'm not a fighter. I never was. I didn't want to do it, but the man-child kept pushing me. *Kick his ass. Don't let him talk to you that way. You can kill that guy.*

Looking back, I recognize that he was actually bullying *me* in this instance, even though I didn't fully realize it then. I didn't want the man-child to bother me anymore, so I got in the other kid's face and pushed him. I started making fun of him and pestering him. I didn't know this kid had the balls, and yet he turned around and punched me. The fight lasted about two and a half seconds, and was the first and only fight of my life. It was stupid. I bullied this kid because if I didn't, the man-child would think that I was a fraud. That I didn't belong with the cool kids because I didn't fight. And that would mean I wasn't valuable. I wasn't special. I would be just like everyone else.

It was hard to see at the time, and it makes me wonder who I bully today. Not in a physical way. But in more subtle ways, without even knowing it. The question is, *Who am I trying to make small so I can feel bigger or worth more?* The guys I work out with? Am I pushing the newer guys and encouraging them to go harder or lift more not for their benefit, but so they see me as an athlete or stronger/faster than them? Am I sharing my story to help my clients, or to show off how far I've come? Am I being rude and not listening to my parents because I'm an adult now and they can't say shit? Or am I protecting myself, speaking my truth, and setting healthy boundaries? Am I using someone's love for me or the relationship to manipulate or control her life in any way?

I believe I've been guilty of all of the above. Not in an intentional way. But nonetheless, bullying is bullying, and I have been a bully as an adult. We all have.

Who am I trying to make small so I can feel bigger or worth more?

If you're a bully, it doesn't mean you are bad. It means you're trying to prove your value, and it's time to break that cycle so you actually build real value. If you don't, you're just peeling your own scabs. Take the power back by taking responsibility for your actions and how they impact others.

I was treating a kid for addiction when I was working in a nonprofit residential facility. He was a big boy, muscular and aggressive. He wrestled, played football, and fought any chance he could. He had testosterone coming out of his ears. I didn't want him as a client because he reminded me of the bullies who would beat kids up during the weekday, then steal their dad's car stereo on the weekend. I didn't want him because, honestly, I was afraid of him. Since I never got physically bullied growing up, I never learned how to fight. He was seventeen and I was in my thirties, and he could no doubt put me on my back in three seconds. But he got assigned to me. So I counseled him from a distance. I knew that if I could befriend him, he would be cool with me. Not get in my face. Then over time, I got to see a different side to him. He got persuaded to dance in our annual talent show. He went from street fighter to dancer in a boy band. And he loved it. But he was self-conscious. He didn't want people to think he was a "sissy", especially his father. I got to see a side to him he never showed before. He was just a kid who sought approval, validation, and acceptance. Then I met his father. Holy fuck. I heard stories of him beating up three grown men at a Tommy's Burger while mom and son watched from the truck. Not back in the day. Like, a year ago. He was the kind of man people in prison would be afraid of. Anyway, his dad had a problem with his son dancing: "My son's not a pussy." I was suddenly in a pickle. Everyone was looking at me to get his dad's approval for his son to dance, including the son—my client. How do you get someone who puts people in the hospital for staring at his wife wrong to change his definition of man?

I invited him to watch his son at dance practice. Of course he didn't want to come, but I eventually convinced him. He came begrudgingly, stood right next to me, stone-faced. I told him how much progress I'd seen with his son and how his new love for dancing was helping him move away from his addiction. I said, "Look how happy he looks up there." He couldn't deny it. He saw that his kid was just a kid and how happy dancing made him.

And as we started to connect, he shared a story of how his dad used to beat him daily. It was like he was looking at himself on that stage. And in that moment, he realized that his distorted definitions of man had come from his father's distorted definitions of man, and that he'd passed them down to his own son, leading in part to the boy's pain and addiction.

So, he let his son dance.

Something *his* dad never gave to him.

#8
Don't Whine

It wasn't until I was in my mid-thirties that I realized I was a whiner. I had just discovered CrossFit. The workouts were grueling, especially if the workout had a movement I wasn't used to, or one my body didn't necessarily enjoy. So if I came in and the workout wasn't in my wheelhouse, I complained and bitched about it for the entire warm-up, all the way up until the clock was set and it was 3 . . . 2 . . . 1 . . . Go time. People laughed because they thought I was just being silly John Kim. But I was dead serious. I was indeed complaining about the work that needed to be done and my desire to do it—even though I had shown up voluntarily. When I started training with a small group of athletes, though, I realized something. I was the only one who would complain. No one else whined like me. They might make one or two comments about it. But then they just did the work.

It was a defining moment. When you realize you're *that* person in the room.

Then I started thinking about my past. When my dad used to take me and my brother to work, I would pout the entire time. From the ride to the office to the ride back. Non-stop. If I wasn't whining with words, I was doing it with my bratty behavior and negative energy. Ten hours of complaining. Looking back, going to work with my dad were the worst days of my life. And yes, no kid likes to do manual labor—pulling telephone cables in cubicles. But the thing is, I wasn't a kid. I was in my twenties. And if I had had a better attitude, hadn't complained and whined and brought myself and everyone else down so much, the experience wouldn't have been as bad as I made it. I know, you're thinking, *Going to work with your dad were the worst days of your life?* No, of course I've had more challenging days. But because of how much I resisted and fought and pouted, the imprint of those experiences was straight-up traumatic. My brother, on the other hand, only a couple years older but raised under the same roof and torn from the same cloth, never complained. Not once. He went to work with my dad twice as much as I did. They brought me along only if they needed extra help. Was it easier for him because he was stronger or had more physical ability than me? Nope. I was in much better shape than him. The only difference was our mind-sets. One of them belonged to a boy.

> **As men we have a responsibility for our own happiness. Whining and complaining only make a bad or difficult situation worse.**

Then I started thinking about my relationships and if I was whiny in them. No surprise: of course I was. Behavior ripples. If you're whiny at work or in the CrossFit box, you're probably whiny in other areas of your life as well. Okay, so I'm just going to cut to the chase and give you the most embarrassing example. I don't think I've told anyone this. I was in my early thirties and married. We weren't having much sex at this time due to our relationship drifting. This one night I really wanted to have sex. She didn't. I remember lying in bed, flipping and tossing my body around wildly. It is almost comedic as I think back on it, like a *Saturday Night Live* skit. A thirty-year-old man flopping around in bed like a fish out of water because he didn't get what he wanted. I'm pretty positive it prevented her from sleeping, and most likely kept her up wondering what kind of twelve-year-old she had married. Sexy, right?

As men we have a responsibility for our own happiness. Whining and complaining often are the result of us not taking responsibility for that. The example above about me whining because I didn't get sex wasn't about sex. I was whining because I wasn't happy. I was whining because I wasn't where I wanted to be in my career. I was whining because I didn't like myself. I was whining because I wanted someone else to fill my empty spaces.

What do you whine and complain about most often? Your job? Your boss? Where you're at in your career? Your girlfriend not doing things you want her to? Or the way you want her to? How much money you're making? Your body? Your family? First, ask yourself if you're generally happy. Or if, like I was, you're a miserable fuck. If it's the latter, your constant whining is a sign that it's time to change yourself and your life so you start taking responsibility for your happiness.

#9
Don't Peer over the (Metaphorical) Urinal

At a young age we discover our penis and become fascinated by it. Although it's always been there, we are suddenly intrigued and curious. We can't take it apart, so we start playing with it. We realize it gives us pleasure, a new and exciting sensation. It makes us feel powerful. Subconsciously, we begin to associate penis with power.

Middle school hits, and the requirement to change for gym class alerts us that penises come in different sizes. Our power is now compared with other boys' power. We go from feeling like Superman to Clark Kent. Now we're taking an object and internalizing it to determine our worth. This thought pattern brings us anxiety and makes us feel less than. It is a pattern many young men struggle with, and then continue to struggle with as they go through life.

Then we discover porn and the massive penises that come with it. Now we're not even Clark Kent. We're the intern at the *Daily Planet*, pushing mail carts and dodging staplers. Since changing our size is not an option, we try to make up for it in other ways, in the classroom, at work, and on the court. Or with cars, houses, and year-end bonuses. And then, of course, with women. Soon we're comparing everything we have to what other men have. We become workaholics, alcoholics, and can't get it up anymore from all the stress and anxiety. We lose the very thing that once made us feel powerful.

I've been insecure about my penis since I can remember.

Those examples above aren't random. My insecurity started in locker rooms, comparing myself to other boys. Then I discovered porn, and it put lighter fluid on my insecurity. When my marriage was falling apart in my thirties, I blamed my penis even though my wife assured me she didn't have a problem with it.

It wasn't until I was in my thirties and dating a girl from Georgia that my outlook changed. She was the first woman after my ex-wife who I expressed my insecurity to. She told me about the guy she had dated right before me, a giant Irishman with a baby arm between his legs. One would think this would only make me feel more insecure about myself. But she went on to explain how she hated it. It was too big. She couldn't do anything with it. "Sex was always painful," she told me. Of course there was a part of me that was like, "Come on. You're just saying that to make me feel better." But that was programming from watching the women in porn pretending like they can't get enough of these giant men. She was being honest. She said my penis was "perfect". Or at least, perfect for her. No one had ever said that to me before. It was the first time I felt like I was okay.

> REMIND YOURSELF, NOBODY'S BUILT LIKE YOU. YOU DESIGN YOURSELF.
>
> – JAY Z

Recently, I started dating someone who told me on our first date that she once broke it off with a guy she really liked because his penis was too small. She didn't just blurt this out. We had a few drinks and were on the topic of sex. Of course, this instantly triggered that old insecurity of mine. But after a few dates we got intimate, and there were no complaints. The axe didn't drop. She still wanted to be with me. More importantly, I started to discover other things that I hadn't before, like the importance of touch and the art of kissing. Discovering bodies with a new lens. I became a student to love and intimacy, and everything felt like the first time. Except this time it wasn't just about skin. It was about connection and energy. Things you can't see.

I learned that there is so much more to intimacy and sex than the size of your penis. There is no magic in your wand. Your power lies in a different organ: your heart. And if your lover is not satisfied with your size, you are with the wrong lover.

We all come in different shapes, sizes, and colors, and that's what makes us beautiful and uniquely us.

We all have insecurities when it comes to our bodies. For men, maybe their penis or hairline. For women, their breasts or thighs? But if we put weight on those features that we don't like about ourselves, we will begin to tie our worth to them. Then we will feel less than because our bodies don't look like what we believe they *should* look like. And of course our shoulds come from advertising, which isn't real. Our buy-in gives our power away to external factors. This can become an obsession. We take desperate measures to "fix" ourselves, to chase an image we've created in our minds. But it is just a Band-Aid. You may start to look like the model in the magazine, but you will never heal the real pain—feeling insignificant, unworthy, unlovable inside. To stop this process, we have to stop comparing ourselves with others. That is the leak. That is the opening that allows us to bash ourselves. We all come in different shapes, sizes, and colors, and that's what makes us beautiful and uniquely us. We must realize that our differences aren't what's lacking in us but rather are what makes us valuable. What does noncomparison look like in your life? What does it look like to toss your ruler? Or maybe keep the ruler but just start measuring different things, like your ability to make someone feel safe, sexy, and beautiful. Because then they will do the same in return, and you won't find yourself needing to compare yourself with anyone.

#10
Don't Be Nice, Be Kind

Most people think "nice" and "kind" mean the same thing, but there's a huge difference:

Kind: Kind comes from the heart. It is pure, without strings, without conditions. It is genuine positive regard. Kind is gentle. Kind is a gift. Kind is compassionate. Kind is good-hearted. Kind is sympathetic. Kind is giving.

Nice: Nice comes from an approval-seeking mind. Nice is usually a product of insecurity. Niceness is good manners, in exchange for a reward. Nice can be processed. Nice can be lined with fear. Nice can be false. Nice can be forced. Nice is a negotiation.

You know that saying "Nice guys finish last"? It's true, but not because people are shitty and walk all over good dudes. Nice guys finish last because their focus on constantly pleasing others makes it impossible for them to find their own truth—their voice, opinions, values, beliefs, and story. You can't possibly find those things within if you are always seeking approval and validation from others.

In high school, I had a crush (ever think about the double meaning in that word?) on someone who rejected me because I was too nice. Now, I understand high school isn't real love and a sixteen-year-old getting shot down is a normal part of adolescence. But there is a takeaway here that applies to adults. Anyway, her name was Jennifer, and I had been crushing on her for, like, two years. And two years in high school is like ten in real life.

One night at a party I was drunk and emotional. My eyes were watery from crying in the bathroom about my so-called life. She noticed that I had been crying and pulled me into the hallway to ask me what was wrong. Her energy was different. She pressed her forehead against mine as Violent Femmes' "Blister in the Sun" was playing in the background. She pulled me in. We kissed. The world stopped. I couldn't believe it. From that night on, I followed her around like a lost puppy, hung on her every word, gave her a sweatshirt and a Social Distortion cassette tape. Then she started fading, and I couldn't understand why. Finally, I heard through a girlfriend that she thought I was "too nice". I was fucking pissed. What did she want?

Here's the takeaway I learned years later as an adult after many more crushes and relationships. It wasn't really that I was too nice. She wanted me to be *somebody*. I cared what everyone thought, especially her. I was like a leaf. My gifts and concern for her came from an approval-seeking place, not a place from within. I exchanged my truth for member-ship.

Now, let's get one thing straight. Giving Jennifer that cassette tape could have been a kind gesture. But it was the way I did it that made it people-pleasing and nauseatingly nice instead of a normal gesture of kindness for a girl I really liked. My motive in hanging on her every word wasn't so she would feel heard; it was so she would like me. And therein lies the difference between niceness and kindness.

A nice man can practice empathy, forgiveness, and con-gruence, but a kind man can do this without sacrificing his self.

When you think about being nice versus being kind, start questioning your motives. Kindness comes from a place of truth; niceness is a negotiation. Whenever you are doing something for someone—giving a gift, your ear, your time, whatever—is your intention to give or to take? Are you giving this because you want something in return? Acceptance? Approval? Validation? Or are you truly giving without conditions or wanting anything back? Are you giving to satisfy your flawed sense of self? Being nice. Or are you genuinely giving your gift without wanting anything in return? Being kind.

People pleasing.

When you are constantly trying to please others, you start to lose your sense of self. You may not be aware of it because it's a slow burn. And it's not something you just wake up one day doing. It runs deep. You laid the tracks when you were younger. You learned early on that by pleasing others, you received love and acceptance. You felt valuable. So you kept doing it to feel worthy. Eventually, the self takes a back seat and whoever you're pleasing—mom, dad, women, friends, boss—takes the steering wheel. You start to live outside-in instead of inside-out. You lose your voice. Your uniqueness. You feel unheard. You build resentment. You have no sense of self.

It's impossible to build a true sense of self-worth when you are constantly trying to please others.

#11
Don't Just Wear the Compassion T-Shirt

L ike "gratitude", "self-care", and "namaste", the commercialization of wellness has turned the word "compassion" into a popular meme. So let's take a giant off-line step back and revisit what compassion really is.

Here's my definition of compassion: a desire for others' suffering to be relieved. Compassion is a state of curious caring. Compassion is empathy: to clearly see the nature of what someone is going through. When you are compassionate, you are pulling from a place of wonder, not judgment. Compassion is presence. You have to be in the moment to be compassionate. Not thinking about bills, weekend plans, or what you want for lunch. Most important, compassion is the willingness and desire to see beauty in another. This is the big one. We all have stories, with certain chapters we want to rip out, lined with guilt and shame. To be compassionate toward someone is to see beauty in their story, to shed light on their darkness. Compassion is kindness.

As men, we are taught to be driven and aggressive—to win at all costs. Compassion is extra. It's charity. It's not something we should be focused on daily. For many, it's a weakness, not a strength. It means we have to put down our shield. Be vulnerable. Be a martyr.

So instead of compassion, most young men set their sights on the other C word—competition. We are fighters, providers, problem solvers—and we have to be better than everyone else at what we do. What happens when men are constantly pinned against one another in competition? We lose our ability to be compassionate. And we sacrifice our power because of it. Yes, there is healthy competition. But when your mind-set is locked on beating everyone at everything, it puts you on an island. Competition separates us. Compassion unites us. Turn your dial to Compassion. That is where your true power lives. It will get you off the island and onto the team.

Here's the thing: our power lives in our humanity. In Buddhist tradition, they talk about having a strong back but a soft front. However, many men display so-called strength in not showing themselves and not opening their hearts. Instead of having a soft front and a strong back, many of us have a defended front shielding a weak spine. This is called posturing. (For more on posturing, see p.24: "Don't Be a Double Douche".)

> IF YOU WANT OTHERS TO BE HAPPY, PRACTISE COMPASSION. IF YOU WANT TO BE HAPPY, PRACTISE COMPASSION.
>
> – DALAI LAMA

Practicing compassion allows you to lower the shield, yet keep your spine and your back strong. The place where these two parts of your body meet is where courage, compassion, and our true strength live and grow. Competition is exhausting. But compassion doesn't drain us. It empowers us.

Compassion is more than support. You can't truly champion someone's story if you are not compassionate toward him or her. Let's apply this to relationships. (This is just dipping our toes in. We'll fully dive in in Part Three.) Ask yourself, *Do I support my girlfriend's/wife's story?* Of course you do. But then are you compassionate toward her? Without compassion, support can turn into control. True men feel deeply what someone is going through, without judgment or placing their own definitions on them. Because that's selfless and giving. That takes effort and heart. True men go *with* their partner, not *at* them. They hold a space that is safe and unloaded. And do what they can to help with another's suffering without losing their self. Boys, on the other hand, try to fix. They make it about them. They don't have the ability to hold a safe space. They think caring about someone means losing a part of themselves. Then they expect something back for that sacrifice.

Without compassion, support can turn into control.

When you practice compassion, you not only share your unconditional love to help another; you strengthen your own soul and become even more open to receiving love back. You grow in soul and spirit, become a conduit for love. You turn from a stone to a prism. You reflect energy and thereby get more back. Fuck competition. That's the real win-win.

#12
Do Seek Nectar

I used to be obsessed with chasing rainbows instead of finding joy and meaning in what was in front of me. I was absent in relationships and constantly in my head. I wasn't in life. I was in line. Being in line makes you powerless. You're like a muzzled greyhound chasing a dangling carrot around a track. You'll never catch it. You're not meant to. So all you do is chase. And chasing makes you powerless, and feeling powerless makes you angry. Sound familiar?

Not to be clichéd, but it wasn't until I started focusing on the journey instead of the destination that I became happier. By "focusing", I mean this: *accepting everything that is in front of you—your relationships, your situation, your divorce, your money or lack of it, your shitty job, your painful transition, your whatever you're dealing with or going through.* Then leaning into it and trying to build something from it. Meanwhile, stop obsessing about what you don't have, and try to produce joy from what you do have. You can have yachts and mansions and that company you've dreamed about building, but if you don't have the ability to produce joy from what's in front of you, you will never be satisfied. You'll always want more. You'll always be chasing. Happy will always be an island you're trying to swim to.

So I got out of line. I accepted my situation and went back to school. I changed careers. I started a blog. I bought a motorcycle. I started to find joy in small moments. Writing blog posts. Hugging canyons. Sweating in a CrossFit box. I was done chasing. This was my life, and I was going to make the best of it by leaning into my journey and finding the gold. I realized that life is not about waiting. It's about seeking, discovering, learning, growing, and in this process producing joy. *Because happy doesn't fall into our laps. We must produce it.* It must be squeezed out of what we have in front of us. We must wade through all that is manufactured, programmed, and contrived. Break monotony by wearing new lenses, ones that allow us to explore edges and find truth. In moments. In energy. In human exchange. Seeking nectar means to simplify, look closer, and find life in your life.

Today, I have a hummingbird tattooed on my left bicep as a daily reminder to seek nectar. Always. It doesn't have to be expensive things or life-altering experiences. I mean, it can be. But that's easy and obvious. What's important is one's ability to produce nectar from the mundane, the daily. It's like in relationships—how so many of us put importance on sex and sexual chemistry. But 90 percent of a relationship is just hanging out and doing nothing. Life is the same. Most of life is in simple moments. It's finding a happiness that fills those moments that is key.

Seeking nectar means to simplify, look closer, and find life in your life.

Here's the funny part. None of these are new things. I've always had these. They've always been in front of me. Even when I had "nothing". I just never had the ability to find joy in them. I was too busy chasing more. But today I can find joy in them, just as they are. And that's what I believe separates a man from a boy. His ability to produce nectar.

It starts with a choice. To see gold sprinkled throughout the rainbow instead of in a giant pot at the end. Then a call to action: practice finding it. Every . . . single . . . day. Like a muscle, you have to exercise it. Until one day you have the ability to produce joy no matter what your circumstances are. This is when you take the power back.

**Here is a sampling of the nectar
I am able to produce today:**

Meaningful conversations with friends and clients

My first cup of coffee in the morning

Writing

Revelations about myself

Five seconds of dopamine after a hard workout

Riding my motorcycle

Cooking

Socializing with friends

A good film

Meeting someone new / hearing a new story

Night walks (alone or with someone)

Days at the beach

Feet in the sand

Sun on my back

A breeze on my face

Naps

Meditation

Creative expression making videos

Trying new foods

Breakfast for dinner at a hole-in-the-wall diner

Kissing mindfully

So, stop waiting in line. Stop wasting your gifts. Seek joy, always, in everything you do. It doesn't matter if you're doing the dishes, going on a date, or building an empire; this mind-set will allow you to be open and aware, to unlock yourself so that you can unleash your gifts. The world needs you. You were meant to change it.

HEALTH

As you know by now, CrossFit changed my life. It was a physical manifestation of my internal transformation. Yet when I talk about health, I'm rarely talking about exercise. In fact, as you'll learn in Part Two, health is about feeding our internal selves with external practices, not about having a perfect body or going gluten-free.

So much of a man's health is about taking time for self-care. Why do we only ever hear women talk about self-care? We need to change that. Because having a healthy lifestyle isn't about doing biceps curls in front of a mirror or taking a weekend off from alcohol. Activities like traveling, meditating, and full belly breathing should be part of every man's vocabulary. Seeing your friends for meaningful "man dates" and laughing like you mean it are part of having a healthy relationship with your friends, your body, your job—and yourself.

Do Sweat Daily

HEALTH,
in a shot glass:

Men sweat daily. Men breathe deep. Men do more than wish and worry, wish and worry. Men go on man dates. Men aren't trapped in their own head. Men travel. Men dance. Men prioritize the things that make them feel alive. Men don't take themselves too seriously. Men laugh unapologetically. Men eat fucking vegetables.

#13
Do Sweat Daily

Humans used to wake up at dawn and spend the day hunting for their dinner. We used to build our own homes, fetch our drinking water, and cut our own firewood. We used to make things with our hands. It gave us a sense of accomplishment. We used to run, climb, swim, jump, and sweat. And it wasn't called exercise. It was called life.

Today, we cruise in air-conditioned cars, ride elevators, and sit in cubicles. We build equity, climb the corporate ladder, and cut corners. We resemble robots more than we do our earlier ancestors. But sweating reminds us that we aren't machines or hamsters on a loop—that we are in fact human, and we were made to move.

There are obvious health benefits to sweating. It flushes out toxins and disease. It can also aid in improving cardio-vascular health. As the body heats and produces sweat, the heart works harder to improve circulation. By regularly working up a good sweat, we get long-term health benefits. But that is not the reason I believe men should sweat daily.

There's a privilege in tasting our own salt. It reminds us that we're human. It gives us a different sense of worth than landing a promotion or closing a deal. It exists on the most basic human level, one stripped of external forces, involving nothing but you and what God has given you. It's our way of shedding. The result of sweat is a shot of empowerment. This stimulates self-esteem, crushes false beliefs, and generates testosterone—all imperative in the journey of man.

It's not just about the sweat.
It's about the reunion with self.

But most importantly, sweating is a way to connect with your body. Many of us played sports, skated, surfed, raced dirt bikes, wrestled, and break-danced while growing up. (Well, maybe the break dancing was just me!) As we got older, we disconnected with that part of ourselves because jobs, girlfriends, mortgages, utility bills, and, well, life happened. Some of the happiest times of my life were when I was a twelve-year-old spinning on cardboard. I felt whole, invincible. As I grew up, I disconnected with that part of myself.

I'm not saying my forty-four-year-old self should start break-dancing again. I mean, maybe. What I'm asking you to do in sweating daily is to connect to your spirit, the you that is you at your core and nothing else. I found that spirit through muscle-ups (see p.212) and handstand push-ups in CrossFit. And that connection made me feel whole again. Complete. Found. It's not just about the sweat. It's about the reunion with self. And if you've never played sports or never did anything active as a kid, your daily sweat will be about an introduction to that part of yourself you never knew. Both take you to the same place: a better, stronger version of you.

#14
Do Calm the Fuck Down

Yes, everyone including your mother has been telling you to do it. But you've tried and haven't seen any results. You've seen the talks. You've read the articles. But *it's not for you*. You've tried it and it didn't take. Anyway, what does calming down have to do with being a man? After all, you want to be a man, not a monk.

First, let me share my journey with trying to calm the fuck down. I've always been a spaz. I was the loudest kid in the classroom. And then at recess and on the playground, a mile a minute with everything I did. I never learned how to breathe. Everyone would tell me to "relax"—which, if you're anything like me, is just a trigger to flip out more. Then I grew up. And nothing changed. I couldn't put my phone down. I was thinking of ideas when people genuinely wanted to know how my day went. I wasn't present with people I cared about. I was always on the go. Never at home. Go-go-go. But when you're an adult, you can't live like this, running around like your head's cut off. You burn out. More importantly, though, energy spreads. Not being able to calm down affected my brain. I would be in my head all day, drowning in my thoughts, which led to poor sleep, tight shoulders, and feeling like an exhaust pipe. It was difficult to be productive and present with my clients. I needed an escape from myself.

So I tried to calm down by meditating. *Really* tried. I didn't want to tell my clients, who also drown in their thoughts daily, "Do as I say, not as I do." I downloaded apps. I took video courses. I tried guided and unguided. I sat on pillows, lay down, tried everything save attending a silence retreat in the woods somewhere. I was afraid to do that. I was afraid I wouldn't make it back, as in I'd probably lose my mind. Then I'd have to change everything to "The Crazy Therapist". Anyway, none of it was sustainable. It didn't work for me.

And then something clicked. I decided to commit to meditation like my workouts. I didn't give myself any excuse to skip. I put it on my priority list, next to riding my motorcycle and doing CrossFit. I lay down, closed my eyes, and focused on my breath every day for fifteen minutes. It was rocky in the beginning, but I didn't judge each session as successful or unsuccessful. I just got them in. That was my goal. Then I moved it up to twenty minutes. It's been a couple of months now, and finally I'm noticing trees and shit. No joke. I mean, I don't see auroras, and I still sink in my own mental quicksand some days. But it has helped me distance myself from my thoughts. It has helped me put a speed bump between my thoughts and my actions, which helps me respond instead of react—one of the things you'll find on p.87, where I list things that I believe make a man. Again, energy ripples, so the calming of my mind also helps me calm my body. And in that process, there is a connection. That's the true gift of meditation. It connects you to self, grounds you. When you are connected and grounded, you are more present and have more clarity. (And you can get out of your own head.) You need this space/silence to see your life better. So you can make better decisions. You can

> ## WORRYING IS STUPID. IT'S LIKE WALKING AROUND WITH AN UMBRELLA WAITING FOR IT TO RAIN.
>
> ### – WIZ KHALIFA

detach from feelings that usually suck you under. Anger releases its vice grip, and your creativity opens. If you aren't grounded and connected, you're just a walking reaction —pulling from panic and all your cognitive distortions— which was me for most of my life. Meditation is about more than stillness. It's a doorway to raising your human potential.

I lay down, closed my eyes, and focused on my breath every day for fifteen minutes.

You don't have to open your third eye. You don't have to sit on a cushion in a cave. You just have to sit still and focus on your breath for fifteen minutes a day. But every . . . single . . . day. You must commit to it. Make it a priority. Because there's something at stake. The person you could be.

#15
Do Slingshot Yourself into the Present

The most powerful way to slingshot yourself into the here and now is to practice mindfulness. I understand that "mindfulness" is a buzzy word with a million meanings. Like meditation, we hear about its benefits and the new lenses it can give us, but who the fuck's got time? Well, you don't have to sit somewhere by yourself or set a timer for this one. This is something you can thread into your daily life, in everything you do. It's a mind-set. But here's the thing: Results don't come instantly. It requires time.

When I look back on my thirties, I remember the stress and the pressure. I remember wanting things, the panic and desperation. And I remember the pivotal events that happened like plot points in a movie. But I don't remember the actual moments or the feelings. When I look back on my twenties, I remember more specific scenes. The breeze on my back while catching sun in my parents' backyard in the Glendale hills, while my girlfriend was swimming in the pool in front of me. The feeling of grabbing my pants seams on the beach at 3 a.m. while being yelled at by the pledge master. And as I look even further back at my teenage years, moments in time and feelings get even more specific. The first time I got head, the sun piercing the room, the sound of my friend's voice as he was telling us we had to go and I was screaming inside, Nooooooo! This is the best feeling of my life! Onstage, dancing with half the high school football team in a talent show. I remember exact voices. Expressions on faces. The applause from the audience.

Going back further, when I play back my childhood, there are pure flashes I remember as if they happened yesterday. Legos. Break dancing. Thanksgiving at my friend's house with his *Brady Bunch* family. The fear and exhilaration of throwing full soda cans out the window of a station wagon as we were going to the beach. The world felt so big.

The reason I remember more moments the further I look back at my life is because the younger I was, the more mindful and present I was. Yes, there is the fact that when we're young, most of our experiences are new. So the imprint is deeper. And of course we were more curious. But we also weren't thinking about our credit-card bills and how to scale our company. We were fully present and engaged.

As I grew up, I lost my sense of wonder. I stepped out of life and into my head. I lived mostly in the future, wishing and worrying. Wishing and worrying. Wishing and worrying. Stuck in a mental and emotional loop. That's why I don't remember as many moments. And if I do, they're not as rich. I know they happened, but I don't remember the feeling; it's more like a list. It's like I started losing my senses and saw the world only in lines and logic.

The good news about going through a divorce or a time when life strips you of everything and forces you to start over is that you start noticing things you hadn't before. I mean after the panic and realizing that you're not going to die, of course. After you get a job and some direction. After you make some new friends and can actually get out of bed. When your world explodes and you no longer have to worry about what you were worried about before, like how you're going to save your marriage. You are given a new set of lenses.

After my universe exploded, I stood in front of Michelangelo's *David* in Italy and cried. The old me would have glanced at the statue and wondered what I was going to eat

Mindfulness is about an outlook, an appreciation of the world and your place in it. It's a practice that snaps you into the present and allows you to actually live instead of just exist. It isn't about sitting on the floor and meditating. It is an activity that can be threaded into your daily life.

The best way to practice mindfulness is to hang it on an activity. When you're eating, don't inhale your food. Instead, chew slowly. Take in the taste, texture, color, smell—use all your senses. Eat like it's your last meal. When you're working out, don't just focus on reps and weight. Be fully present by noticing your body and your connection to it: your breath, what hurts, what feels good. Notice the feeling of the weights in your hand, and challenge yourself to push through the discomfort. When you're kissing someone, let it be more than just a gateway to sex. Notice the softness of her lips, the shape, the energy, the dance. Kiss like it's your last time. Pick one activity to hang mindfulness on. Then build on it until mindfulness comes naturally as a way of life. The world will brighten.

Here are some things I do daily, weekly, monthly, and yearly to help myself appreciate the moment and get more mindful:

1. **Daily:** Get up early. Notice the morning. Walk to a coffee shop, not drive, taking in the sky and trees. Journal. Write for me (not for work). Create a space for my thoughts, ideas, and feelings to swim.

2. **Weekly:** Seek a sunset, sunrise, mountain, beach—any form of nature. Take off my shoes and walk in the sand, on grass, dirt. Swim in the ocean. Connect to the earth.

3. **Monthly:** Travel, even if it's to a different nearby city. See something I've never seen before. Taste something different. Meet new people. Do it with an open mind and curiosity, as if you're an alien visiting earth.

4. **Yearly:** Do something that scares me. Maybe an activity like swimming with sharks in a cage or starting a new project. Try to take it in mindfully instead of panicking. Notice everything, and allow mindfulness to eclipse the fear.

for lunch. Instead, I just stared and soaked it in. I remember the details of all the buildings on the streets, standing like works of art. The feeling of the cobblestone sidewalks on my feet. The warmth of the Mediterranean Sea, and how different the water felt than the Pacific. Of course I was traveling, so naturally I was going to notice details and remember moments. But it didn't stop when I got back to Los Angeles. The fear and calm of riding a motorcycle for the first time. The feeling of burying my feet in the California sand, which I've known for my entire life. But this time it felt different. Like it did when I was ten. I started noticing trees and how the palm trees here are all slanted. I noticed my thoughts. My breath. My energy. I actually tasted food instead of inhaling it. Not since I was a kid or teenager did I use all my senses like this. I didn't know it at the time, but I was practicing mindfulness. And I stepped out of my head and into life.

And it made me a better man.

I paid attention to people. I listened better. Made eye contact. I was more present. I was kinder. I was more forgiving. I was more pleasant to be around. I became more creative. I started to enjoy life. I stopped being a boy.

If you don't practice mindfulness, you will always be a spinning hourglass on your frozen computer screen. Reboot yourself by practicing mindfulness; make yourself three-dimensional.

You don't need to go through a major life event like a divorce to start practicing mindfulness. You just need to commit to putting on that new set of lenses and then start appreciating the moment.

#16
Do Get Out
of Your Bubble

Most people leave home when they graduate from high school. They go away to college, a different state, a different country; they study abroad. If not, they leave to pursue their dreams after college. Move to a big city. Hollywoodland. The Big Apple.

Not me. After high school, I lived with my parents and commuted to a university thirty minutes away. Then after college, I helped with the family business as I pursued screenwriting.

I guess I can blame it on my culture, since Korean children are expected to live at home until they get married. The truth is, travel wasn't important to me. I saw it as recreation, as extra, as play. If you leave, you're wasting valuable time. Someone else is getting ahead while you're buying souvenirs. My ambition kept me in a bubble.

Beat.

Okay, the real truth is I was afraid. I was scared to leave my little cocoon. I was afraid to explore the unknown. Go on my Hero's Journey. Slay dragons. Return different. Finally, at thirty-seven, I took the plunge. I traded my "motorcycle money" for two weeks in Italy and Spain. I figured if I got the bike first, I might not have legs.

This trip was my little ice-cream-shop taster spoon of travel. I had pizza where it was invented. I stood in front of art I had learned about in textbooks. I rode scooters. I swam in the Mediterranean. I saw beautiful people. I had conversations with strangers. I met a girl. I walked. I danced. I drank. I explored. I lived.

Travel will open your mind, stretch your heart, and allow you to see.

Any opportunity you get to travel, just fucking take it. Life doesn't give us an invitation to go anywhere. We have to make it happen. Don't wait like me to get your taster spoon. Order a cone, a giant waffle cone. It will be filled with knowledge, perspective, acculturation, substance, discovery, and growth. It will open your mind, stretch your heart, and allow you to see.

Another thing: men who travel have more practice with patience. The act of travel can be tedious as hell. Flight delays, broken-down buses—not to mention the difficulty of dealing with other cultures, sensitivity, communication—require one to strengthen the patience muscle. Men who travel have a better understanding of people. They experience other languages, rituals, cultures, societies, foods, music, art, business, living, and production. Men who travel are more open. They have the ability to adjust, adapt, see the world through other people's eyes. A well-traveled man is a wise man.

17
Do Eat
Something Green

My journey with food has been a rocky one. My parents owned burger stands and fast-food franchises while I was growing up. Fried chicken for breakfast. Egg rolls and chili fries for lunch. Tacos for dinner. Fast food was always just a "call before Mom leaves" away. This meant two things. One: I had a lot of friends as a kid. Two: I formed an unhealthy habit that would lead to many heated arguments later in life between the adult and the child sides of my mind.

Today, I still struggle with my desire for all things processed and fried, but it doesn't have the control over me that it once did. I have learned to tame my desires, to not let my wants overthrow my needs. I have finally learned the concept of control. Simply put, I have become a grown-up in the kitchen.

**A man's diet is a direct reflection
of his self-control, discipline, and
how much he loves himself.**

Diet is an often-overlooked aspect of life that distinguishes the men from the boys. Boys consume what tastes good. Men also eat what tastes good, but they focus on what is *good for them*. Eating solely what tastes good is a reaction, not a response. It is an impulsive action. Eating what is good for you requires thought and discipline.

It is a response to your body needing nourishment. There

is maturity in that decision and strength in the ability to execute it.

That being said, all in moderation. There's nothing wrong with pizza and milkshakes as long as they're not the only things you consume. Balance is key. A strict diet where you beat yourself up over one Cheeto isn't really acting like a man either. This is less about food and more about self-love and self-care. It's about respecting your body, your whole self. Yes, eat mindfully. Eat greens. But have a fucking doughnut once in a while and be okay with it. Respecting your body also means giving yourself what you desire, but in moderation. A man's diet is a direct reflection of his self-control, discipline, and how much he loves himself. Suffering is just as unhealthy as stuffing your face.

So let's just say you eat Doritos for breakfast and pound Mountain Dews for every meal. Great. Let's focus on what you can do to start taking control of your diet. You like sugar. Who doesn't? The goal is to change your palate. Not beat yourself up. This takes time. But once you do, Mountain Dews will taste like pure syrup and you won't crave all the shit you used to. First, set the intention. Then slowly start threading a new diet into your life. Junk food is like a drug. You can't quit cold turkey. Wean yourself off gradually. Be easy on yourself. You will fall off the wagon many times. But remember: This isn't a race or competition. It's a transformation. I tend to focus on three things:

1. Eating mostly foods that come from the ground. This means real food, nothing processed. No chemicals.

2. Cooking meals like I'm cooking for someone, even if it's just me. This way you see exactly what you're eating, and consuming food isn't just unwrapping a wrapper.

3. Being spontaneous, trying new things, and learning something new about food every day. Take a baking class.

Get lunch at that weird vegan place down the street. Go to a food-truck festival and try one of everything. Visit your local farmers' market. Buy a cookbook and make everything inside.

You don't need to identify as a "foodie" or start making crepes. You just need to start caring about what you put in your body. Turn it into a lifestyle, because men don't thrive on junk food.

#18
Do Laugh Hard

There are two types of people in this world. People who laugh, and people who laugh *hard*. I am neither. I can barely produce a smile. I've always hated the way it looks. I had jacked-up teeth growing up because I was too cool to get braces. So I grew up being the "I smile with my eyes" or "I laugh on the inside" guy, which is just another way of saying "I'm insecure!" The truth is, I hated that I couldn't laugh like everyone else, that I didn't have the courage to start.

I've learned that laughing isn't just about laughing. When you don't allow yourself to laugh hard and fully, you are blocking yourself. You are saying to yourself that you can be only *this* happy. You can express only *this* much. You are limiting yourself. And every limit is lined with shame. Shame will always keep you a cardboard cutout. By allowing yourself to laugh, fully—no matter how insecure you are about your teeth, the sound of your laughter, or whatever it is that's preventing you from laughing without restrictions— you are scrubbing away the shame. You are saying, "I'm good enough, I matter, and I don't give a flying fuck what others think. I am me. Watch me laugh." You turn from two-dimensional to three-dimensional and remind everyone else that this is what life and being human looks like. And that is sexy AF.

Today, when I feel that delicious trembling and my face starts to open, I remind myself to commit like a gymnast doing backflips. I push through, let go, and laugh as hard as

I can. Because I've learned that laughter is life. It says so much about your attitude and ability to be happy. People who laugh hard live in the moment. They seek nectar. They are spontaneous. They are adventurous. They are committed. They are courageous. They are confident. They are displaying vulnerability. They are showing the world they can be confident and happy without announcing it. They are expressing themselves and choosing to share it with others, which allows others to feel something. They are spreading joy. They have a thirst for life. They are leaders.

People who laugh hard live in the moment.

So if you're going to laugh, do it fearlessly; life is too short to just smirk.

#19
Do Things That Make You Feel Alive

The five seconds after crushing a workout where you pushed yourself harder than you ever have before. A life-changing conversation. Makeup sex. Catching a wave for the first time. Standing on the edge of something. The company of a beautiful woman. Swimming in the ocean, naked. Revelations about yourself. That moment when she kisses you back. Seconds before your first marathon. A fresh broken heart. Hugging canyons on a motorcycle. The birth of an idea. The moment you realize you're in love with someone.

The difference between feeling good and feeling alive is fear. We are not afraid of things that make us feel good. A safe job, a comfortable relationship, twenty minutes on a treadmill. These things don't require much effort. We are not scared of them. But if you want to feel alive, there must be an element of fear. We might get injured. We might lose money. We might be rejected, labeled, or fired. We might be wrong. But with risk comes reward. Feeling good is not enough. It keeps us trapped in a bubble. *Good falls into our lap. Alive doesn't.* If we want to feel alive, we must seek it or we will start to feel dead. Feeling good isn't enough. We must feel alive.

The monotony of your daily life combined with the pressures from work and relationships can put you in an emotional coffin. If you want to break out, you must seek what pumps blood into your heart. From the moment you wake up to the second you fall asleep. Little things, big things—it doesn't matter. It's not about the activity. It's about the process of facing your fears.

Get out of your fucking comfort zone.

Ask for that first date. Stand up to your boss. Publish a book. Start a blog, a company, a movement. Pick up a guitar. Eat something you otherwise wouldn't. Go somewhere you've never been. Get out of your fucking comfort zone. Explore your edges. Turn your dial from Good to Alive. This stretch will change your life. Shatter the fishbowl you live in. Stop swimming in your own shit. If you're content with good, content is all you'll ever be.

#20
Don't Take Yourself Too Seriously

When we take *what we do* seriously, we are honoring our gifts. When we take *ourselves* seriously, we are announcing that we *are* the gift. Instead of standing behind a podium, we are stepping onto a stage. Unless your gift is to entertain, no one wants a show.

Taking what you *do* seriously is leading, excelling, and making yourself and your community better. It is giving.

However, taking *yourself* seriously is seeking attention, not leading by example, and taking energy and resources from the people around you. Boys take themselves seriously; they take and don't give. *If a man is confident in who he is, it will be reflected in what he does.* To reach your maximum potential, both must occur. So the next time you feel a need to put on a show, use that energy to *produce* good work instead of to *perform* good work.

You may be wondering what this discussion is doing in the "Health" part of this book. Taking yourself too seriously means you have an unhealthy relationship with you. There is posturing and ego. You are pulling from a place of having to prove yourself, which means you are insecure. If you focus on taking what you do seriously instead of taking yourself seriously, you are realigning the relationship you have with you. You are now focusing on your gifts, which will make you more of a whole person. Simply put, you will like yourself more and not feel the need to take yourself so seriously. And this new relationship with yourself will ripple through the relationship you have with your body, your job, your family, your friends, your love. Boys have something to prove because they need approval. Men let their work speak for itself.

A note to the women out there reading this.

If your man believes he is better than others, he probably believes he is better than you and this relationship. I don't say this to hurt you, but to wake you up to reality. It's only a matter of time before this kind of narcissism and "taking" creeps in and starts ruining things. But this is not just about you or the relationship; it's about doing your part to help turn boys into men so that your potential son will grow up with mentors instead of bullies. Call his bluff. Check him. If you don't, who will?

It's also important to note that it isn't women's responsibility to "fix" men. Given all of the bullshit we put women through, I don't want to give women one more thing to worry about. But I do want to note that in my practice and my own story, I've found that we do most of the stupid shit we do because we're seeking women's attention and affection. You are likely the most important thing in his life. If he is suddenly taking himself too seriously and becoming a narcissist, is it potentially rooted in your relationship? Is there a way to shut that down without killing his self-esteem? Yes: change the dynamic of the relationship, and people in the relationship will start to change. You do this by practicing transparency and telling your man how you feel, how his actions and mind-set are affecting the relationship. Nothing will get a man who loves you to look at himself more than letting him know that the chemistry is changing.

#21
Do Dance (Especially If You Don't Know How)

I have personal experience with this one, and I'm sure you do, too. Put us in a situation where we may look foolish, and our response will show how comfortable we are with ourselves. Ever since we were kids, men have been programmed to capture the flag. Our competitive streak is etched with permanent ink. If we believe we can't do something, we tend to avoid it. The "dancing flag" sits very high on a steep mountain that most men aren't willing to climb. Not that we don't want to. But fear of looking stupid (failure) keeps us from embarking on that journey.

It's about getting comfortable with the uncomfortable.

What people find attractive isn't your ability to do head-spins or a fancy Charleston. If you can, great. They will be entertained, as they would if they were watching a good magic trick. But they won't be as impressed as if you danced without knowing how. One requires talent, but the other requires courage. And this ability to be brave, to not care what others think, is what is sexy.

Of course, dancing isn't the only activity that brings discomfort to men. But I do believe it's one of the most common and challenging. Encouraging yourself to dance, especially if you don't know how, isn't about capturing a person's eye. It's about getting comfortable with the uncomfortable. It's in this space that we find growth.

22
Do Go on Man Dates

As I roll up to a red light, he pulls up right next to me, pops his helmet window open, and says casually, "She doesn't like going down on me." I pop my face mask up and yell, "I don't blame her." He flips me off. We race to the next stoplight. I open my face mask and reply, "She doesn't trust you." I slap my helmet mask down, pop the clutch, and shoot forward.

The next stop is frozen yogurt. We sit on the ledge licking our giant waffle cones like kids allowed to hang out alone for the first time, our motorcycles parked right next to us. Now the conversation is about work and our frustration with our careers, where we are now versus where we want to be. We express our fears in ways only men understand. The night ends with bear hugs. We leave lighter than when we arrived.

When women go out, it's less about the activity (unless it's dancing—half joking) and more about the connection and spending quality time with each other. When men go out, it's always about the activity. The football game. A workout. Barbecuing. This is because we are doers. Not talkers. And yes, doing does form a connection. For example, my most memorable man date to date was with a group of men riding dirt bikes from Sequoia to Yosemite. We were on motorcycles and in our own thoughts for most of the trip for ten days. But if it hadn't been for the raw honest talks around the campfire each night, the kind of chats we don't usually have at work or the gym, the trip wouldn't have had much meaning. Vulnerability is where the connection is truly formed.

When women go out, they are vulnerable. They talk about all the shit that's going on in their lives. Their conversations are meaningful and sometimes life-changing. Then they dance that shit off with mimosas. And I think we can learn from them by mixing activity with raw authentic conversations where we truly show ourselves. Because sharing our state is where humans exchange lives.

I've hung out with men most of my life. Bike races. Frat parties. Workouts. But it wasn't until my mid-thirties that I started going on man dates, having real, meaningful conversations that men don't usually have because we are not vulnerable with each other. Conversations about love, relationships, failure, fears, frustrations, and our feelings. Because, as stated at the beginning of this book, men are more likely to suffer alone and get to a place where they actually take their lives—not just have suicidal thoughts like women. For example, take breakups. We all go through them. But they are tougher on men because they get all their emotional support from the women in their life, and have less of a strong social network. We don't talk to other men about our breakups. Instead, we isolate. We have less of a social network to help each other because we haven't laid those tracks. Meanwhile, women are surrounded by love, understanding, and, yes, "Let's get you drunk" friends. If you rely less on your lady for every single one of your emotional needs, you will bring more of yourself to every relationship, and have a stronger foundation to stand on.

How to do a man date:

1. Don't make it weird.

2. Mix the activity with real conversations.

3. Do it often.

#23
Do Do Things Alone

Growing up, I spent my days break-dancing, skate-boarding, racing bikes, and chasing girls. All social activities. My mind was programmed to do things with others, so when I became an adult, it carried over. Movies. Parties. Motorcycle rides. Fitness. All with friends. I never did anything alone—until I got a divorce.

The divorce threw me into a world of solitude. Not by choice. I didn't have many friends then because my life revolved around my wife. (See previous chapter.) I hadn't made an effort to make friends until after we got married. Big mistake (one that many people make), because they were mostly her friends. I was just the husband. They weren't friendships built on me. They were friendships built on us but first through her, so when we separated, they defaulted back to being her friends, not mine. So I found myself alone for the first time in my life. I remember lying in bed on a Friday night and, for the first time in my life, not having one single person to call to go out. Not one . . . single . . . person. It was more than sad. It was strange. I was Tom Hanks, on an island talking to a volleyball. Except I didn't even have a volleyball.

I didn't know it at the time, but it turned out to be a blessing. It forced me to get to know myself, get comfortable with myself—to grow, to become a man.

I went to movies by myself. I sat in diners by myself. I went on motorcycle rides by myself. I went on walks. Runs on the beach. Hikes. I watched sunsets. I did everything you

> **Being alone versus being lonely.**
>
> The stronger your alone muscles, the less likely you will be alone.
> Because people gravitate toward people who can sit by themselves.
> Who can do their own thing. Who don't need to be with others to
> exist. Who actually like themselves.

would do with a friend or an intimate partner, but by myself.
And it was uncomfortable. I was lonely. I felt self-conscious.
But I knew this was part of my rebirth. So I leaned into it. I
pushed pass the discomfort and sat with me.

After the unease and loneliness, I started to get to know
myself in a way I hadn't before. I saw myself outside of
myself, instead of from inside my own head and insecurities.
From this position, there was less self-judgment and more
self-curiosity. Not just "What does John like?" but "How
does John feel, and why?" Did I start speaking out loud to
myself in the third person? Maybe. But that's another thing
that's great about being alone—you give less fucks.

You know that saying "You should treat yourself as you
would a good friend"? Well, that's what I started doing. I
started to be kinder to me, accept me, embrace who I was.
That's the piece that makes spending alone time so crucial
to your journey as a man. It's not just about getting to know
you. There is a tipping point once you spend enough time
with yourself: you start to like you.

As important as it is to spend time with our friends,
girlfriend, wife, coworkers, and family, we must also spend
time alone. Overtime at work does not count. When I say
alone, I mean things that allow you to know and discover
yourself. The world calls it "me time". I call it any activity
that clears your head, resets your body, and reboots you as an
individual.

Many men define "me time" as golfing with Dad, having a beer with the boys, or taking a trip to Costa Rica. But we don't do those activities alone. Women, however, are experts at "me time"; they enjoy the process. It's a mental bath. They crave it. They need it. It brings them comfort; it puts them at ease. Which brings me to the more important piece of doing things alone: Feeling comfortable with ourselves affects other areas of our lives. It builds confidence. We will seek less from others and have a stronger sense of who we are. We won't have to cling to our partners at a party.

When's the last time you went to a movie by yourself? Ate dinner in a restaurant alone? Went out on a Friday solo? And—this is important—enjoyed your own company? If you feel discomfort when you are doing things alone, explore it. Where does it come from? Do you feel self-conscious? Are you worried about what others will think of you?

When these feelings creep in, remember: Doing things alone doesn't make you a loser. It makes you healthy. It makes you attractive. It makes you whole.

LOVE AND RELATIONSHIPS

So by now I've made it pretty clear that my divorce was the turning point of my life. And my divorce stemmed from a terrible outlook on love and relationships. Maybe that makes you wonder if you should be trusting me to give you advice in this department.

No, you shouldn't. You shouldn't trust anyone. Because we're all fucked up, have different stories, and we can't push our definitions onto others—especially when it comes to love and relationships, because there are so many factors. But my hope is that there is something in my story you can relate to, and possibly learn from, just as there are things in your story that others can learn from.

So here we go.

LOVE AND RELATIONSHIPS, in a shot glass:

Men don't react; they respond. Men do the dishes because they want to. Men don't call women fat, ever. Men express love as an action, not just a feeling. Men couldn't care less about their partner's sexual history. Men love hard.

#24
Do Respond,
Don't React

I love my dad. The older I get, the more respect I have for both of my parents, who came to this country barely speaking English, put food on the table for me and my brother, kept a roof over our heads, and gave us an education and designer jeans. As a provider, my father was an excellent man. And Dad, if you're reading this or listening to it because it's been translated into Korean (I hope it will be because these kinds of conversations are sorely needed there), I want you to know I love you and this book would not be possible without you. I have learned from you a strong work ethic, humor, and a good kind of inappropriateness that reminds us we're all human. And those elements have given me a voice. That being said, this book is about my definition of man, and I gotta use you as an example here to show one of the greatest differences between a man and a boy. It comes down to responding versus reacting.

My father was a walking reaction for most of my life. There was no pause between how he felt and how he behaved. He would come home and vent on the family. The sky was always falling. He didn't have the tools to hold back. Instead, everything was a reflex. When he was angry, we knew. When he was stressed, we felt it.

As I got older, I stepped right into my dad's shoes, a walking reaction. Especially in my relationships. I would lose my temper, talk over people, and vomit my negative energy without considering how my state would impact others. If I felt discouraged and frustrated, I would put it on them. I call it "emotional littering", and I dumped trash everywhere. It wasn't until I went through many relationships, including a marriage and subsequent divorce (have I mentioned that yet?), that I understood the importance of responding instead of reacting.

Responding is a form of taking responsibility. By choosing to respond instead of react, you are taking care of your own shit. You are saying, "I *feel* this way but I choose to *act* differently because it's healthier. Because it will create a safer space for others. Because life isn't just about me." This ownership makes you a man, and a whole lot more attractive.

> **Responding is a form of taking responsibility. By choosing to respond instead of react, you are taking care of your own shit.**

Here's the thing: No child enters adulthood unscarred. We've all been through some form of trauma. My dad grew up making his own shoes and having plates thrown at his head for stealing rice. We've all been bullied, rejected; something has been taken from us. And we did our best to survive our dysfunctional upbringing, life's turbulence, and heartbreak. That trauma threatens to keep us locked inside who we are instead of who we could be. We all have a responsibility to break this lock. With a sledgehammer.

Boys react and men respond. Life tends to have gray areas, however, and the difference between a reaction and a response isn't always obvious. Let me give you an example . . .

Scenario: You get home from work, where you had a weird, stressful day that left you feeling kind of shitty, and your girlfriend—let's call her Sarah—is two glasses of wine deep and playing loud, annoying pop music in your apartment. She's tipsy and in a great mood, and normally you would match her mood, but today the whole thing is irritating. When you walk in the door, before you even put your stuff down, she looks you in the eye and says, dismissively, "What's the matter with you? Lighten up." This hurts your feelings. It also makes you feel incredibly angry, irritated, and alone.

What reacting looks like:

"What the fuck are you so happy about?"

You toss your things on the couch, beeline straight to the bedroom, and slam the door.

You did exactly what you felt like doing without considering how your words and actions might impact your girlfriend. And chances are, you'll be sleeping on that same couch you just tossed your things on.

What responding looks like:

"I'm sorry, baby. I'm having a bad day."

You lean in and give her a quick kiss.

"I love you. Give me two minutes to unwind and I'll join you."

You toss your things on the couch and disappear into the bedroom.

You set your own feelings aside for a second because you didn't want to ruin her positivity and mood but you also were honest and told her how you felt. You gave her a kiss and reminded her that you loved her. But you also drew a boundary and gave yourself the space you needed by letting her know you needed some "me time".

You will be sleeping in bed with her tonight, and I'm sure she will listen to why you had such a shitty day.

We react from pain. Someone insulted us, broke our heart, bullied us, took away our voice, or our self-esteem, or our sense of safety. This hurt encourages us to behave without a filter. It's our way of protecting ourselves. Or so we think. Reacting is actually self-disruptive behavior. When we react, we are not creating a space to heal. Instead, we are passing on our pain. The result is arguments that quickly turn into wildfires, character assassinations (more about that on p.104), and failed relationships.

On the other hand, a response requires thought, patience, and a plan. A response means thinking of the best way to speak and behave in a given situation, one that will serve to heal instead of destroy. This takes work. It means practicing metacognition and empathy, biting your tongue and/or swallowing your ego. It requires examining your feelings, tracing them back to what's under the surface, and communicating that effectively. The result is resolved conflict, increased trust, and strengthened relationships. When we respond, we don't just deflect our pain or frustration. We understand it, which gives it less power. When we react, we are picking scabs. When we respond, we are applying ointment.

#25
Don't Put Your Shoulds on Others

I had a client once who came to see me but didn't know why. He had had a great childhood. He had a great life. He was in love with his wife, had two beautiful children, a vacation home in Santa Barbara. He was self-made and passionate about what he did. He was wealthy, driven, felt a sense of purpose and meaning. He couldn't understand why he was so unhappy.

After multiple sessions, we realized he felt extremely alone and powerless in the world even though he had a "solid" relationship with his wife and kids and a thriving company. After many more sessions, we realized why he was feeling this way. He judged everyone. He judged people on what they wore, what they drove, how they lived their lives. He judged strangers. His family. His employees. And, of course, himself. Harshly. He had a very specific idea of how the world should look and how people should behave in it. And since reality didn't match his blueprints, he felt alone and disconnected.

Once we discovered this, his world cracked open to reveal the truth. As it turned out, he didn't *really* have a healthy relationship with his wife. She walked on eggshells and pretended like everything was okay when it wasn't. He wasn't close to his kids. His employees didn't know him and didn't want to. They worked for him hoping the company would go public one day so they could cash out.

We chased the strings of his judgment down, and they

ended up in a pool filled with fear. He judged because he was afraid. If people didn't fit into his ideas and definitions, it exposed something flawed about him and his perfect world. It meant he was wrong, had done things wrong, had chosen the wrong path or placed value on the wrong things. It meant his world was false and his house of cards would come crashing down. Judgment, then, was his way of protecting his world. It was his way of holding a shield, creating a shell, putting himself in a bubble. But the truth is, he was only fighting with himself. Creating his own anxiety and resisting his own joy.

Once he realized this, he made a choice to stop judging. It didn't happen overnight. It took months. I coached him on making nonjudgment a daily practice. After nearly a year, this is what happened: He started to work less. He and his wife got couples counseling. His employees actually started talking to him like a real person. He had a better relationship with his kids. I started seeing wrinkles in his clothes. (Which, in this case, was a good thing.) He became a real person. All because he judged less? Of course not. There was a shit ton of other work. But deciding to not judge was the first domino. Practicing nonjudgment is what opened the door for him.

If we make a decision to stop judging, and do it on a daily basis, our world opens up. We go from narrow to wide, and in that open space there is soil for compassion, love, connection, creativity, and endless possibilities.

The energy of judgment leaks from your body and pollutes the air. It shows in your face, your eyes, and your fists.

When we judge, we come in loaded. We are stamping a giant "should" on whatever person, experience, or situation we encounter. This is poison in relationships, because every "*should*" is lined with control. It may not be direct. But the

1. Pull from curiosity.

You can't judge and be curious at the same time. When you feel judgment coming on, turn your dial to Curiosity. Wonder why someone is doing or saying what they are doing or saying. Don't label it and take it personally. Create distance by being curious.

2. Try to understand before trying to be understood.

Most people try to be understood before trying to understand. If we try to understand first, we will be a whole lot less judgmental. It leaves room for us to see things how others see them. There can be overlap. Reliability. Understanding. And when that happens, judgment fades almost instantly.

3. Learn people's stories.

We judge people on their words and behavior. But those words and behavior stem from their stories. So if you learn their stories, you will understand why they did or said what they did. You may still not agree with them or be hurt by their words and actions, but this understanding will make it easier to not judge.

Remember, you are not giving someone something by not judging them. You are allowing yourself to be free.

controlling, judging energy is there, and others will feel it. If you want to create a safe space in your relationship, be aware of when you are judging: what she wears, what she eats, who she is friends with, how she lives her life. If she wants opinions, she will ask for them. If not, don't disguise judgment as how much you love her. Love does not come with judgment. "I love, therefore I judge" is not a thing.

You want less anxiety in your life? First, notice every time you say "should", either out loud or, more importantly, mentally. Stop judging everything, everyone, including yourself. Especially yourself. Stop judging your stuff, your hair, your house, your weight, your moments, your relationships, your experiences, your path, and your life. Even if you don't announce it, the people in your life feel it. *You* feel it. The energy of judgment leaks from your body and pollutes the air. It shows in your face, your eyes, and your fists. You are making things about you, and no one wants to be around that kind of person. Judgment does not promote growth. It stunts it. When you judge, you create your own prison. When you accept things as they are, you free yourself and everyone around you.

#26
Do Say "I Was Wrong"

When I was married, my wife and I were invited to have dinner with a wealthy man who had financed the last film she was in. I was a struggling screenwriter at the time, and he was looking for a screenwriter to write a new movie he had in mind. My wife was reluctant about the dinner and said she'd go only if I didn't try to sell myself as a screenwriter. I understood and promised I wouldn't pitch myself. But I told her I'd bring a few of my scripts as writing samples just in case he wanted them. *Writing samples are like business cards.* It would just be a friendly dinner. I could tell she didn't feel comfortable about it, but she said okay.

From the second we sat down at the fancy restaurant overlooking the ocean to the moment we said our goodbyes, I did nothing but try to sell myself as a screenwriter. I talked about my projects. What I'd sold. What we had in common as immigrants who came to America, which he didn't agree with. I was desperate. I needed the work. My marriage was on the rocks. I couldn't lose this opportunity. Getting this writing gig meant I would be bringing something to the marriage—money. And that meant I was a man. At that time I had no income, and it made me feel like a pud. So my manhood was at stake. But the truth is, it wasn't about manhood. It was about my insecurity, feeling less than as a person. I put that above a promise I had made to my wife just hours before.

As you can imagine, the drive home was uncomfortable

to say the least. The tension was so thick you *couldn't* cut it with a knife. Then words came out, followed by emotions, and suddenly we were in a full-blown fight. It was one of the worst fights we had because I didn't admit I was wrong. I was in pure defense mode. I spit out all the reasons why my actions were reasonable. *We needed the money. It was a great opportunity.* I even spun it and told her that if she was a good wife she would have supported me. But the truth was, I was wrong. I had made her a promise, and then I broke it. Plain and simple. The whys didn't matter. And if I had just admitted I was wrong, yes, she would have still been upset, but there would be more hope. A chance. A conversation. A space to forgive and rebuild. When someone doesn't admit they're wrong, it leaves the other person stranded. You put them on an island. There is nowhere for them to go.

Men who can't admit when they are wrong are basically refusing to grow. In every relationship, if you're not growing together, you are growing apart. So if you won't admit it when you're wrong, it's just a matter of time before your partner feels as if she's outgrown you. Plain and simple.

Swallow your pride and admit it when you are wrong. Discuss it, process it, use it to improve yourself and strengthen relationships. Every time you are wrong, there is an opportunity for growth. Our fear of looking stupid or less than prevents us from this growth.

If you can't admit it when you are wrong, you are unable to reflect. Without reflection there are no revelations, and without revelations all you have are false beliefs and white knuckles. Don't allow your false self, the part of you controlled by ego and fear, to steal this opportunity for your evolution.

Look, if you're going to apologize, then really apologize by saying the words "I am sorry". So many men think they're apologizing, but they're really not if the words "I'm sorry" never come out of their mouths. Instead, a lot of excuses and why you did or said what you did. That is not an apology. That is an explanation. It doesn't matter how gentle or soft you are. You could be crying for all I care. If you don't say you're sorry, your apology is half-baked. You're allowing ego and pride to stand in the way of your heart. It goes back to ownership. If you're going to own it, own it and say you were wrong, you made a mistake. You. Are. Sorry. If you don't, you're ending your apology with a giant "but". And a "but" cancels out your apology.

Let's break it down, since no one teaches us how to apologize.

Scenario: she is mad at you for something.

1. **Step one.** Hear her. Like I mentioned before, try to understand before trying to be understood. More on this later. Literally repeat what she just said. Not in a patronizing way. In a sincere way, so she knows she was heard. For example, "So what I hear you saying is you are mad because I talked to my ex at the party." She replies, "Yes, it hurt me. I understand you guys are good friends now and were before I met you, but it seemed like you were flirting with her." *This* is the fork in the road. You will want to be defensive, because you weren't flirting with your ex. You guys were talking about business. But that's the wrong road, one that many take, and they end up digging a giant hole both people fall into and can't get out of. The right road is to first address her hurt. *Apologize* for it: "Yes, I understand how that could have made you feel. I am sorry I hurt you." Put a period after that. No buts. No "What you don't understand is . . ." Just a big fat period.

2. **Step two.** Now she feels heard. This means there is more room for her to listen to your explanation. Now you can explain your intention and what the conversation was about. But do it gently, with care. You're not in a courtroom arguing your case.

3. **Extra credit.** Figure out how you're going to improve. Stop resisting. This is more for you than her. Do you want to be a stronger human with more tools or not?

   Tell her you'll be more sensitive to her feelings and be aware of them the next time you engage with your ex. Note: You don't have to say you will never talk to your ex again, unless that is what she wants. If that's the case, that's another conversation. You have to explore if that's fair to you and if that's something you are willing to do without holding anger and resentment.

4. **And lastly.** Remind her of how much she means to you, of what this relationship means, and that your heart belongs to her. And no one else.

Boom.

She was heard. Her hurt was addressed. You apologized. You guys understand each other better now, and the "fight" made you two closer.

The other thing you are doing—what most men don't think about—is that you're modeling what a real apology looks like. You're showing her how you want her to fight as well. You'll be making your relationship bulletproof.

Remember: Admitting when we are wrong isn't a sign of weakness. It is a sign of strength. It takes courage to acknowledge our mistakes, defects, and shortcomings.

Make "I was wrong" (or, if it's easier, "You were right") your new superpower.

#27
Don't Be
the "I Dunno" Guy

As men, we never want to be wrong. If we're wrong, it means we have failed. We've lost. And since we tie our worth to our performance, we are wrong = we failed = we are less of a man. So we put a lot of weight on making the "right" decision. So much so that sometimes we don't make a decision at all. But making decisions takes courage. And it's *that courage* that makes a man. Not whether he is wrong or right. It's the ability to execute, to choose, to put something in motion.

Have you ever gone out to eat with someone who can't decide what he wants to order? He goes back and forth. Back and forth. He asks, "What are you having?" which is normal. Then asks the server what's good or popular. Again, normal. But after ten minutes or so, when he eventually asks the server to just pick something for him, it's no longer an indecisive thing. It's a character thing. This is the same guy who doesn't know where to take his girlfriend on a date. The guy who enjoys "all music". The guy who doesn't know who to vote for. Can't tell you what he liked or didn't like about the movie. He's the "I dunno" guy and never has an opinion. He doubts and second-guesses himself. He can't make decisions. His inability to pull the trigger blocks his journey from boyhood to manhood. Men make decisions. You have to, or you can't build anything. Or lead anyone.

Ambivalence repels love and trust like flipped magnets. Without the courage to decide, no one will follow you. And

How to ditch "I dunno", or how to find your voice.
It's really simple. I started asking myself what I wanted. But more importantly, I made a promise to myself that I would express what I wanted, and do my best to give myself that. Building self-esteem is about holding on to the promises we make with ourselves. We become the "I dunno" guy because we don't have self-esteem or self-worth. We don't believe we matter. The way you stop this pattern and finally find your voice is to give yourself one. Promise yourself you will express your wants and do everything you can—of course, without hurting others—to give yourself that. Without guilt, shame, and everything else that will try to kick in because you're not used to doing it. Like all self-betterment, it's a practice. But it starts with a promise. And every time you break it, you are puncturing your self-esteem balloon.

in relationships, it will stunt chemistry, attraction, and growth. *She may not agree with your decision, but she must trust that you have the ability to make one.* Without this ability, there can be no relationship. She is seeking a man on a mission. Not a boy lost at sea.

I was the "I dunno" guy in many of my relationships. If you asked me what I wanted for dinner, I didn't know. If you asked me what I wanted to do on the weekend, I didn't know. I didn't know because I didn't have a strong sense of self and thought it would be easier to just let someone else make the decision. But not giving yourself a voice deteriorates you. You start to dissolve like Michael J. Fox in *Back to the Future* when he couldn't get his parents together. He literally started to turn invisible in photographs. That's what happens when you "don't know" for too long. People don't see you anymore. But more importantly, you don't see you anymore. It wasn't until I started to make decisions—it didn't matter if they were wrong or right, if I picked a lane, declared my opinions, allowed myself to be heard—that I started to live instead of exist.

Your decisions will define your character.

The ability to make a decision is a skill. It allows you to build trust, pave a road, accomplish goals. The pattern of these decisions will determine what kind of journey you're on. It will remind you of who you are and where you are going. It's better to choose and be wrong than to not choose at all. If you don't pull the trigger, you will lose your gun. So pick a lane, a side, a color. Choose a restaurant, a partner, a cause. Your decisions will define your character.

#28
Don't Pee
in the Shower

Listen: If she doesn't mind you peeing in the shower, sure, go ahead. Write your fucking name on the wall. It's all good and doesn't make you less of a man.

I'm talking here about if she doesn't want you to pee in the shower but you do it anyway because you think she won't know. It doesn't matter how much you follow it down with shampoo. Women can smell that shit. They have a better sense of smell than we do. But this is not about odor. It's about the act of doing something behind their back. It's about trust.

If you lie about peeing in the shower and they know you're lying or suspect it, chances are you are lying about other things. Maybe not big things. But lies don't have to be big to crack trust. Peeing in the shower is one of those "what else" behaviors. *If he's doing this, what else is he doing?* Are you feeding the dog under the table? Riding your motorcycle without a helmet? Flirting with the babysitter?

Peeing in the shower isn't about peeing in the shower. It's about white lies and the way they can slowly disintegrate trust and eventually relationships.

I used to pee in the shower all the time, even after I agreed that I wouldn't. I did it because I thought it wasn't that big of a deal and there's no way she's going to find out anyway. It turns out women are gifted detectives. Even though she didn't make that big of a deal about it, there was a new hint of suspicion in her eyes every time she questioned me about something. Even if I was telling the truth. And that's what's important. Being a man means cutting out all the white lies that undermine your credibility, no matter how insignificant they may seem to you. It's a direct reflection of your character. If you insist on peeing in the shower, make sure she knows you do it. Don't tell her you won't do it just because that is the easier path. Take the hard path: have the conversation. It will free you from having to keep track of your lies, and will let her know you insist on maintaining a transparent, honest relationship.

> I'M NOT UPSET THAT YOU LIED TO ME, I'M UPSET THAT FROM NOW ON I CAN'T BELIEVE YOU.
>
> – FRIEDRICH NIETZSCHE

29
Don't Tear
People Down

John Gottman, known for his work on marital stability and relationship analysis through direct scientific observation, could predict divorce with over 90 percent accuracy. He spent his career studying how people fight. He discovered that it wasn't about how many times we fight. It was about *how* we fight. And character assassination was one of the deciding factors in determining if a marriage would last.

Character assassination can be malicious, but it can also be minimal. Often, it starts with mocking. When we call someone things like idiot, loser, or stupid, even if we're totally joking, we are slamming their worth. No woman will ever find this funny. No matter in what tone or under what circumstances. I once called an ex-girlfriend a "fatass" in a totally joking manner after she ate a plate of pears I left behind when I went to the restroom. It was a joke. I honestly did not mean what I said. At all. I thought it was no big deal because my brother and I used to talk to each other like that growing up. Little did I know she was struggling with an eating disorder at the time. That one comment created an avalanche of insecurities. I'm trying to think of the male equivalent. Imagine if a woman made fun of your penis. In a joking way, no big deal. Would you think it was funny? Probably not. You would have questions.

So you say, "I was wrong." But here's the thing about character assassination: there is no undo. And if you con-

The boomerang word.

Unless you're referring to your steak, the word "fat" is off-limits. Most women automatically internalize this word. It's what I call a boomerang word. No matter where you throw it, it will always come back at you via her. Even if you were talking about someone else, your girlfriend or wife will assume you're thinking the same about her. It's not worth the fight. Trust me. Eliminate it from your vocabulary. Women and weight. Oil and water. This will never change.

tinue to assassinate her character, she will drift. And you won't even know how far since her low self-esteem / fear of losing the relationship may keep you in the dark or unaware of the damage. This internalization will lead to unhappiness. Eventually, she will seek help to process her anger and resentment. She will begin to have revelations. Her therapist will identify the character assassination for what it is, and send up a giant red flag that this is an emotionally abusive relationship. Her self-worth will rise as her false beliefs dissolve, and eventually she will go through a rebirth. Simply put, she may not have the strength now, but when she does, she will be gone. I know. It's happened to me.

Here's the thing about character assassination: there is no undo.

Know this: There are two things relationships rarely recover from—infidelity and character assassination. When you belittle someone, even if you're joking, it's difficult to recover from. Like with infidelity, she may forgive you. But she will not forget. So if it becomes a pattern, the hairline cracks in trust will add up until your relationship container breaks and there's not enough Super Glue in the world to fix it. The relationship will have drifted too far to turn back.

Poking "fun"?

Boys assassinate character because they don't have enough courage or tools to fight fair. They put others down because of what's lacking inside themselves. Think before you poke fun at people. What's your intention? Is it to make someone feel small? Or truly to connect and share a laugh? If you don't know, assassinate your own character. That's always a safe bet.

#30
Do *Want* to
Do the Dishes

There's a movie called *The Break-Up*, with Jennifer Aniston and Vince Vaughn. They're a couple going through a breakup, and there's a scene where they get into a huge fight and Jennifer explodes, shouting, "I don't want you to do the dishes, I want you to *want* to do the dishes!"

Sometimes we do things because we're supposed to or because someone wants us to. And when this becomes routine, it turns us invisible. It's like we died inside. We become a zombie. You're no longer doing life *with* someone, you're doing life *around* someone, or worse, *for* someone. And the other person, whether it's your girlfriend, best

Word to the wise.

When it comes to dishes and chores and things that need to get done around the house, a reframe may be helpful. You are not helping her when you do the dishes. You are not helping her when you do the laundry. You use the dishes, too. You have laundry also. You are contributing to the house, a shared space. The days of women's work and men's work around the house are long gone. That's an old game that doesn't end well. Toss away gender roles and old definitions passed down from our parents. Your house is your safe tree, your temple, and a direct reflection of what's happening inside. Keep it clean. Set the tone.

friend, or company partner, feels equally alone. Like you checked out. Like you're not there anymore.

Yes, there are things in life we have to do that we don't want to. Paying bills. Washing the dog. And of course, doing the dishes. But we don't do these out of desire; we do them because we don't want to rock the boat, because we would rather just do it than get into another fight, because we want to get it over with. Doing things just because we're told to creates a disconnect with the act, which creates a disconnect in yourself, which creates a disconnect with those around you. Yup, all because of dishes.

Don't sacrifice your truth because you're afraid of conflict.

Do things because you want to. Not because you have to. Do things because they come from your truth. Not your obligations. And if it's going to bring resistance, drama, pushback, be a fucking man and deal with it. Handle it. Don't sacrifice your truth because you're afraid of conflict. Life is full of conflict, and that will never go away. It's your ability to resolve it that will make you a better man.

#31
Do Let Go of Your Partner's Sexual History

et's be completely honest. No matter how much we convince ourselves that it won't matter, knowing how many people your partner has been with will eat at us like an Ebola virus.

The phases below hang on general patterns I have discovered from coaching real men with their relationships. And of course, my own personal story.

Phase one. At first, it's just fun and curiosity. He wonders about her exes. She gives him some information. He starts comparing and asks questions about their performance and maybe even size. But it will come off as half joking (to avoid appearing insecure about his own). So he asks questions in a fun and curious way to retrieve the information without appearing threatening. She won't know it's a trap. Neither will he. He believes he can handle it—but he can't. (He will be paying me for therapy later.) She tells him a few details but nothing more. Because she knows how this will play out. She's been here before.

Phase two. Now he's off to the races. First, in his own head. He begins to compare and compete. Plays imaginary sex scenes from her past based on the little information she has given him and fills in the rest with his own insecurities. He assumes, labels, and judges. This leaks into the bedroom.

Now he's competing. It went from in his head to actual action. There is a disconnect. She's confused. He's angry. She doesn't know why. It's no longer a game for him. He has tied her sexual past to his worth as a man. Now he wants to know details. He has to know: if he is not bigger, then he has to be better. She won't tell him details because she is protecting the relationship. This makes him feel like he's inadequate. He makes it about him.

Phase three. Now he starts to believe she would rather be with her exes even though nothing in her behavior or words leads to that conclusion. But still, he believes it with every fiber of his being. She will think he is "fucking crazy". He will be defensive. And she will realize that he is acting exactly like her jealous exes, which is why she broke up with them.

Don't get me wrong: you can discuss and explore past relationships if your intentions are to get to know your partner's story so you can be empathetic and understand her better. But there's absolutely no reason to know her sexual history. Leave that shit in the past. I don't care how confident you think you are; it will only make you insecure and turn you into a pouty little boy.

At the end of the day, it doesn't matter who she has been with. What matters is that she is with you now. Don't mess it up by digging into the past. It will only break trust. Let it go. Live in the moment.

Remind yourself of these three things.
Plus, ask yourself one question.

1. Know that she is choosing you. It's easy for us to forget some-times that our girlfriend actually wants to be with us. Yes, she had a choice, and she chose you. She is with you now and no one else. This means if she wanted to be with her exes or anyone else, she would.

2. Know that women are wired differently and care more about connection than anything else, and the connection she has with you she's never had with anyone else. This means you bring something unique and rare to the table that no one else on this planet can.

3. Know that it's your insecurity that wants to know, not you. Which is *your* responsibility to work on. Not hers.

Plus: The question: What action are you taking to work on this issue, without blaming her or making her feel responsible? Actual action. Not just thinking about it.

#32
Don't Place Her on a Pedestal

I had a client who did everything he possibly could to be with his girlfriend at the time, even after she cheated on him constantly, breaking his heart over and over again. He would do anything she wanted: gave her ten thousand dollars to help her get her life together and even agreed to move to another country for her even though he didn't want to. He was supposed to meet her there, but his car broke down eight hundred feet away from the border. This was one of many signs the universe gave him. But he ignored all of them. He moved there anyway, and she ended the relationship once again two weeks later. He lost himself and his life, over and over. Every time she broke up with him, he made it his mission to get her back. She was his everything. All he saw.

You may think, *Well, I wouldn't do that. That's not me. That's stupid.* But it doesn't happen overnight. It's a gradual burn, and there are many layers. When you put someone on a pedestal, the relationship dynamic that pulls you toward this person becomes stronger than your common sense.

The deeper layer: My client lost his father while he was with her. His father was everything to him and, apart from her, all he had. When he lost him, she took his place. Now she was all he had. He couldn't go through another loss. So he would do anything to not lose her. In doing so, he lost himself. This caused him to go from her mouth to her nipple. It changed the relationship dynamic. She no longer saw him as a man. She saw him as a boy who would always come back when she wanted. This allowed her to lose respect for him. And when you don't respect your partner, you don't trust him. Without trust, there is nothing. You are building on sand.

I didn't lose my father, or move to another country for my ex-wife, but I did put her on a pedestal. She wasn't a person. She was a beautiful piece of porcelain I put on a high shelf. I didn't believe I deserved her. She was "out of my league", and if she found out, she would leave me. So I would do anything she wanted me to. This combined with my distorted definition that being a "good husband" meant to put her first, always, above everything, including myself, changed the dynamic of the relationship, which I believe was the main contributor to our divorce. I thought that's what it meant to give completely. Besides, love means sacrifice. Right?

Wrong. Love means compromise. Not *self*-compromise. There is a huge difference. In one, you are giving. In the other, you are taking. When you put her on a pedestal, you are creating room for sacrifice, not compromise, entering a long dark hallway where you will slowly lose yourself.

When we sacrifice self by always putting our partner's needs above our own, by doing whatever she says even if it conflicts with our own truth, we are disconnecting, breaking, and seeking something from the other person that we lack in ourselves. We are no longer a wall for her to lean on. The relationship becomes limp.

#33
Don't Stop
Courting Her

This isn't some women's-magazine bullshit. It's a mind-set, one that may save your relationship. I've coached so many men who have lost love because they think it's self-sustaining. News flash: Just because you get the girl doesn't mean your work is done. It's actually just the beginning. Like feeling good versus feeling alive, relationships might fall into your lap, but romance doesn't just happen. It takes effort and creativity. You must fan the flames.

Useful tools: Date night. Love notes. Thoughtfulness. And eye contact with intention. Prove that you remember what she likes. Know her love language and speak it. Demonstrate desire.

I understand. Life happens. We get busy. Distracted. We forget that we need to feel wanted, desired, and valued and don't understand why things have changed when nothing's wrong. What we have to realize is that courting shouldn't turn off when commitment turns on. It is an ongoing process of showing up and proving that you still want her, through action, words, and energy. It is relationship water, and without it the relationship will dry up.

Courting doesn't mean you have to write her name in the sky or buy her fancy things. I mean, it could, but that's not sustainable and, honestly, too over-the-top, which will backfire. Courting can be little things, like love notes, thoughtful cards, flowers for no reason, compliments, noticing little

Kiss like you mean it.

Do you remember your first kiss? Of course you do. You know exactly where you were and what you were wearing. You remember wondering if you should use your tongue, if your braces would cut her, and how long you should keep your eyes shut. But what you remember the most isn't how it went; it's how you felt: the bats in your stomach, the fear in your heart, and your sweaty palms.

Do you remember your 2,123rd kiss? Of course you don't. When we kiss someone new, it's exciting. It's our first time experiencing the other person intimately. We take our time, bathe in it, get lost. Our mind-set is in discovery mode. We are open to explore. Once we're in a relationship, kissing becomes routine. The exploration is over. We use it as a handshake, a hi, a bye, a see ya later. Or a gateway to other things. Rarely do we kiss to discover. We forget the meaning behind kissing. Kissing means to express, connect, validate, assure, give, share, trust, and explore.

When's the last time you got lost in a kiss where you forgot what day it was? Where your neck hairs stood up, and danced? Where the kiss could stand on its own and not need to lead to something more? Where nothing mattered but you, her, and the moment?

Renowned marriage researcher John Gottman recommends a six-second kiss. Twice a day. Why six seconds? Because a six-second kiss has "potential". There's actually room to be mindful, to experience romance and connection. To feel something. A two-second kiss isn't actually a kiss. It's a peck. A pat on the back. How long are your kisses? What's behind them? Are you kissing just to kiss? Or to actually express your love?

things like the nuances of her mood, her energy, the way she wore her hair or the way she smells. Center everything around thoughtfulness. How would you show that you're thinking about her in action? Do that. It goes a long fucking way. It produces Super Glue. *So whatever you did to get her, keep doing it.* It's not a guessing game; it should be easy. You know her better than anyone, and if you don't, you have a bigger problem. Time is not an excuse. Make her feel beautiful and she'll make you feel invincible and vice versa. Relationships are a living, breathing thing. They need to be fed, nurtured, grown. And giving her a ring or kids doesn't give you a free pass.

Remember, you're not chasing or seeking attention. You're validating, expressing, and sharing. You're reminding her why she's with you.

#34
Don't Just
Netflix and Chill

When I was in my twenties and had a date, this is what I would do. I would wake up early like it was Christmas and wash my car. By hand—none of this driving-through-a-machine bullshit. Then I would hand pick the songs I wanted to play and load the CDs into my six-disc changer in the trunk. Then I would go work out so I felt good about myself. Then I would drive to the movie theater to buy the tickets in advance so we wouldn't have to wait in line. (This was before the internet.) And of course, dinner reservations were already made. After getting ready, I would pick her up from her apartment. I would park my car, walk to the door, and knock. Not sit in the car and honk my horn. I would open the car door for her. And if there was a spark and things went well on the date, I'd send flowers or a note or something she could actually hold in her hands in the next few days.

You may read this and think, *Wow, what a loser.* Well, okay. But this process is what made dating fun, exciting, romantic, and fulfilling. It made the date a mini-event, something to look forward to. It wasn't just about the person. It was about the whole date experience. But more importantly, *it gave two people a real chance because effort was put into it.*

Today, a date is a coffee or a drink but not dinner because what if they don't look like their picture. Today, a date is "I'll meet you there." Today, a date is scheduled sex because of the kids. Today, a date is not really a date because there's no such thing anymore.

Dating is dead. And that's my point. It doesn't matter if you're single or in a relationship: we, as men, need to bring dating back.

Why? It will save relationships. It will create new ones. It will turn the engine on so love is not an app.

Why men? Better question: Why *not* men? Taking a woman out on a date is an opportunity to take the initiative, make the plans, and set the tone. To not be the "I dunno" guy. It doesn't matter if you're single or in a relationship. A date is a date. It's what creates space for romance, discovery, and connection.

You can't want a cleaner world and toss your Wendy's bag out your car window. So if you want people to find love again. If you want dating to be fun again. If you want your relationship to thrive. Again . . . then let's save dating by putting some effort into it. By treating people like human beings. By practicing transparency and showing your true self. Then maybe we will *all* have a better chance at love.

#35
Don't Perform
in the Bedroom

J ust as women live with the pressure to be physically
attractive, we live with the pressure to perform. Iron-
fisted fathers, determined coaches, and society's definition of success have convinced us that our worth is
contingent on our ability. By the time we are in the rat race
and paying taxes, we are wired to define our value by titles,
bonuses, and corner offices.

We carry this mind-set into the bedroom. And just as
women have been brainwashed by the media about what
beauty looks like, we have been brainwashed by pornography and locker rooms about what a good lover looks like.
Our drive to achieve combined with a warped definition of
sex and intimacy equals performance anxiety, frustration,
aggression, and, ultimately, disconnection.

Quick question: Do you tie her achieving an orgasm to
your being a man?

I did.

If I couldn't make a woman cum, I felt less than. I felt
inadequate. I didn't think she was that into me. I felt like I
wasn't doing it right. And of course that made me believe I
was less of a man. I didn't take into consideration that every
woman is built differently and that their ability or inability
to have an orgasm may have nothing to do with me. So
instead of connecting, I focused on performance. Because if
I couldn't make her have multiple orgasms, it meant I was
not a real man. Simply put, I was making her orgasms about

me. Not her. And when you do that, you start to perform. And when you perform, you disconnect from her because now you're in your head instead of being present, and the chances of her having an orgasm are now slim to none—and slim just left town.

When you perform in the bedroom, you are making it about you. When you make it about you, you are leaving her out. The act becomes a solo challenge to capture an imaginary flag. Your focus on the scoreboard creates an emotional wall. Instead of intimacy being a shared experience, it becomes a measuring stick. The more you focus on your "stick", the less connection your partner will feel and the more pressure you will put on yourself. It's a downhill spiral. Instead, use this space to share yourself instead of prove yourself.

Don't mistake performance for passion. People can feel the difference. One is taking; the other is giving.

And look, I'm not going to lie. I still feel the boyish tug if I can't make a woman finish. I still get frustrated and tie it to my ability and worth as a man. I'm also forty-four, so it takes more than a breeze, if you know what I mean. (And if you don't, you will.) But today, more than ever, I am aware that sex and intimacy are more about connection than anything else. Everything else ripples from the strength of that connection. I consciously have to remind myself because, like so many, I have also been programmed by porn and locker rooms. I also struggle with seeing everything as a competition/performance, including sex. But I've felt the difference between skin hunger and connection. One burns calories; the other produces magic. One stems from insecurity; the other stems from love.

#36
Do Love Hard

Brace yourself. This one's going to be a long one. Because as men, we rarely talk about love. We talk about business, career, cars, workouts—and sometimes our relationship, but usually only when we've been sleeping on the couch. We don't talk about love. Our struggles with love. How we love. Our definitions of love. So let's dive in now. I'll start.

I never went to Love School. I didn't know what healthy love or unhealthy love was. I would just meet someone I had the hots for and suddenly, bam, it's a relationship. I've been in many in my life. I've been married for five years. Dated her for five years before that. I've been in three-year deals, a couple of two-year deals, a few few-month deals. Now I'm enjoying being single again, shaking my love Etch A Sketch, seeing what happens. (If you don't know what an Etch A Sketch is, just pretend like you do so I don't feel so fucking old.)

When I think about what love is to me now, how I define it and what I want from it, I like to imagine my future girlfriend, who she is, who she helps me be, and what we are together.

A letter to my future girlfriend

YOU
You will not take away my boys (guy friends), my fitness, my motorcycle, my alone time, everything that brought me

joy before I met you. You will not try to change my silliness, inappropriateness, or whatever makes me me that I like about myself but may bring out resistance in you. You will not expect me to be a certain way because you've read my blogs. You will not hold my words against me. You will accept me for who I am, with all my defects and shortcomings. You will understand that I am in process and on my own journey, just as you are on yours. And although we are together, we will both have our own personal paths as well. You will be responsible for your own happiness. I will not be your project. I will be someone you choose to love and do life with. Each day. You will not keep me in the dark or in a box. You will tell me how you feel, even if it's not pretty. You will not pick which friends you will and will not introduce me to. If I'm in your life, I'm in your life all the way. You will not present me to the people around you as better than I am or different than I am because of your own insecurities. You will leave room for me to be me as you continue to be you. You will be my best friend but not my only friend. You will shatter your image of what a couple should look like, how they should act, and what kind of friends they should have, and I will do the same. You don't have to agree or like what I'm passionate about, but you must support me because, whatever it is, it matters to me. You will have to deal with my bed head, my night mouth guard, and my horrible sleeping patterns. And finally, you will scratch my back.

ME

I will take all my learnings in my previous relationships and use them to be the best version of myself that I can be. I will always be honest, never assassinate your character, and take full responsibility for anything I do that's wrong or hurtful. I will listen, communicate, open doors—literally—and create a safe space, knowing that trust is earned. Not given.

I will love you as you are, support you wherever you're at in your journey, and hold your hand through all your seasons. I will stand by your side. I will water my own lawn and work on my own shit. I will be responsible for my own happiness and keep the toilet seat down so you don't fall in in the middle of the night. I will write you little notes, make you stuff, and buy you flowers. We will share books, ideas, and sweat—both in the gym and in the bedroom. I will not try to control you or compete with you. I will not try to "fix" you. I will do life with you, not at you, around you, or for you. I will read your subtext, energy, and body language, not just your words. I will do my best to get the hint. I will consider your story. I will make you breakfast. Not every day. But many days. I will always read your heart and intentions before reacting to your words. I will return texts and messages promptly or as fast as I can. I will protect your name and character and be thinking of you in every decision I make.

US

We will both understand that there will be days when we can't stand each other. There will be days when you will want to punch me in the face and I will want to take the long way home. We will disagree on things, like movies and books, and what to buy at the grocery store. I will forget things. Misplace things. You will run late. Our friends will have opinions of us. We will fight. Maybe a lot. You will shut down. I will wonder. But at the end of the day, we will both come back—to each other. And your head will always fall back on my chest. And no matter how many times we fight, we will always fight fair. That will be a nonnegotiable. And we will be together knowing that we are choosing to be together. Not because of logic, age, or loneliness. Not because we look good on paper or we'll make cute babies. Not because we've already committed to this. Not because we don't want to be alone. But because we believe in us and make a choice every . . . single . . . day to be in this and love each other the best way we know how. Our relationship will not be built on fear, as many are. But like many relationships, ours will also be hard. We will not compare each other to anyone else, including our exes. Any residue we have from our past relationships we will work on individually. It is our own responsibility and what being in something healthy looks like. We will sharpen each other and I will make you feel beautiful and you will make me feel invincible and vice versa. The only thing we can promise is to be honest and love as hard as we can. We both know there is risk. We both know we can get hurt. But we are willing to put that on the line to experience the high notes of something meaningful.

We will build something meaningful and sustainable, taking responsibility for our own shit but also leaving room for magic, and settling for nothing less.

Here's what I've learned. *First, love is not a feeling. It is an action.* Therefore, we must not look at love as something that is given but something that we earn, hone, practice, learn from, work at, and strengthen. Why is it that we have no trouble putting in extra time at the gym or working overtime at the office, but when it comes to working on our relationships, it's a chore? We do it only when we are forced to. Imagine the kind of love we would experience, how many marriages could be saved, and how many children would grow up with healthier definitions of love if we put as much time and effort into loving someone as we do our careers, our bodies, or whatever we spend most of our day and energy building.

How many people say they're going to work on their relationship when everything is going great? Zero. Shouldn't we work harder on ourselves and the relationship as it grows

I have coached so many who stop loving because the feeling has faded. And it drives me fucking apeshit. It's one of the reasons why relationships are short-lived. Of course feelings fade. But loving is a daily choice, and you do it until it becomes unhealthy or it's no longer repairable. And even if it becomes unhealthy, you do everything you can on your end to make it healthy again. That's what it means to love hard.

So what do healthy love and unhealthy love even look like?

Well, every relationship is complicated, and there are so many factors that are unique to each relationship. But here are the broad strokes in a shot glass.

Unhealthy love is being powerless, selfish, and enabling. It has no boundaries. Unhealthy love is contingent. It is immature, irresponsible, and dependent. Unhealthy love is urgent. There is a desperation behind it that produces manipulation and compromise of self. Unhealthy love is a pissing contest, a tug-of-war, a mute silence, and a kickstand. Unhealthy love promotes the false self and stunts growth. It is a drug.

Healthy love is a daily offering. It is a gift. It has conditions that shape the self and strengthen the other. Healthy love is feeling powerful and independent. It is grilled cheese and soup on a rainy day but not every day. Healthy love is patient, kind, and accepting. Healthy love requires a tremendous amount of responsibility, which involves communication on all levels and constant reflection. It is building trust, having faith, and holding a commitment. Healthy love promotes growth and two strong containers. Healthy love is rare. It is a choice.

and becomes stronger, not the other way around? I mean, that's what we do when we get traction in our careers, right? We put more time and energy into them. So if you're going to love someone, fucking love someone. Love her like there is no one else on the planet. Love like it's a job you can't wait to go to every morning. And one where you want to wake up early to do it again. Love without fear, without pride, without judgment, and without expectation.

If you're going to love someone, fucking love someone.

Love is a gift. Not a negotiation. If you are expecting something back, are you truly giving? If you are single and feel you've been unable to do these things in past relationships, loving hard means beginning to explore why.

Whatever your definition of love is, the important part is just to do it, hard.

CAREER AND SUCCESS

My career hasn't been like climbing a corporate ladder at a company. I've never had a corner office or even a therapy couch. It has been more like walking through a jungle, paving a path with a machete—my typewriter and iPhone. There have been highs and lows to the extreme. I have been discouraged, lost clients, found success where I wasn't looking, lost opportunities, had anxious nights, been low on cash, made good cash, eaten ramen for weeks in a row, and then turned around and ordered the steak and lobster.

What I've learned: who we are at work is especially important on the journey from boy to man. I'm going to guess that you flipped this book open and went straight to this section. So often, work success is how men define themselves. You can't be a man if you are entry-level. If you don't have letters after your name. Or you don't make six figures.

CAREER AND SUCCESS,
in a shot glass:

Men own their shit. Men don't throw peas at
the wall. Men build things out of failures. Men
create their own definition of success instead
of following other people's definitions.

#37
Do Own Your Shit

Your shit is your shit. No one else's. Not your girl-friend's, friends', siblings', or parents'. Depending on your upbringing and how you've been wired, other people may have owned your shit for you for a long time, so it will require some effort to take what is yours, pack it up in a bunch of boxes, and bring it with you. But in those boxes is your growth. Until you take full ownership of all your shortcomings, false beliefs, insecurities, and cognitive distortions, and stop projecting them onto other people and the world, you will not be able to reach your full potential. You will only make excuses.

I'm the youngest of two boys. In Korean culture, the eldest sibling takes most of the responsibility. So my brother became my umbrella, protecting me from life responsibilities. He went to work with my dad every day as I launched off ramps and spun on my head. My brother wrote invoices and pulled telephone cable on the weekends. I chased girls. My mom did my laundry. Made my bed. Made me food. I was sheltered, to say the least. So when I got older, I depended on other people. It was all I knew. I didn't have any tools because I was enabled. I never learned how to own my shit—which means taking responsibility of where you are in your life.

So when I got married, I ate out all the time, never made my bed, didn't clean anything, did the bare minimum. I was a half ass. And when you're a half ass, you're just getting by. I never reached for great. You're good with good, and your life consists of crossing fingers and depending on others.

You're complacent. Not striving to be better. You don't learn how to earn anything. You're not living. You're just existing.

My divorce forced me into nonprofit work. Although I wasn't interested in the nonprofit world, I was desperate for an income and it was the only thing I could find before I would hit flat broke. But it came straight from the stars, because it wasn't until I was working at a nonprofit that I started to own my own shit. The irony was that I was teaching teenagers how to take responsibility for their lives, but I was also learning the same lessons myself. The program taught kids how to become adults. Things like accountability. Taking ownership. Putting in work. Accepting who you are and building from that. These were new concepts for them, and also for me. Working as a counselor in a residential treatment center became my own treatment.

At the same time, I found CrossFit and it taught me the meaning of discipline and earning your sweat. Before, I would go into the gym and do some biceps curls in front of a mirror. But CrossFit was about moving your body, and pushing it further than you ever have. It wasn't about aesthetics. It was about holding standards, being accountable for your actions, and building not only a new body but also character.

The combination of going through a divorce, working at a nonprofit, and discovering CrossFit gave me a front-row seat at Man School. At first, there was resistance. The child in me was throwing a tantrum. I didn't want to put in the work. All of the above took a shit ton of effort, physically, mentally, and emotionally. There are no shortcuts when you're recovering from a broken heart. There are no shortcuts in nonprofit work. And there are no shortcuts in Cross-Fit. I was used to running away from hard work and waiting for things to be handed to me. I wanted to go home early. Cheat on workouts. Move on from this divorce. Instead, I stuck with the "program" life presented me. I leaned into it.

I stood strong. I didn't have a choice. Wait, let me correct that: I didn't give myself a choice. We all have a choice to own our own shit. I was sick and tired of being a fucking child. There was no going back.

So I put on my nonprofit uniform every day, made my bed (see p.144), spearheaded groups and family support programs, pushed my body more than I ever have in my life. I learned about who I was and how I thought, started acquiring tools, stopped making everything about me. I examined my character. I owned each and every day, fought through my resistance, and documented my journey. Day in. Day out. And through this process, I started to discover things about myself.

I could actually accomplish things. I could help people. I could like myself. And that's the value in owning your own shit. You start to build self-worth. It is impossible to value your life and yourself if you don't take full responsibility for where you're at. It doesn't matter if you had a shitty childhood. Or, like me, one with no responsibility. It doesn't matter if someone took something from you. If someone broke your heart. Cheated on you. Or you went through a natural disaster and lost everything. It's all part of life, and it doesn't matter what events led to where you're at right now. Where you're at is where you're at. You have a choice. Own it and start building. Or complain and cope in whatever unhealthy ways you cope. I complained and coped for most of my life. Finally, when I owned my shit, I started to build. And that difference is the difference between a boy and a man.

It is impossible to value your life and yourself if you don't take full responsibility for where you're at.

What do you need to take responsibility for in your life right now? What do you need to own? Are you taking full ownership of where you're at in your life? Or are you just doing a lot of complaining, waiting for your handout? What is your excuse to not be where you want to be?

Remember, your shit is your shit. Don't let it be pawned off on your shitty parents, the shitty economy, your shitty luck, or your shitty taste in women. You are the constant theme throughout. And only you can figure out how to take all the shit and make something beautiful.

#38
Do Separate Who You *Are* from What You *Do*

Just as our society ties a woman's worth to her beauty, it also ties a man's worth to his ability. What you can build, how many touchdowns you can score, how much money you can make. I want to set the record straight right now: What you do doesn't determine your true value. Your value lives in your character and capacity. Your heart and your story. Not your ability. But if you believe your value hangs on what you can do, as many men do, that mind-set will keep you powerless and always chasing. More importantly, you run the risk of losing yourself and what you truly have to offer.

> MAN MAKES THE MONEY, MONEY DOESN'T MAKE THE MAN.
>
> – LL COOL J

When you measure yourself against your character, you have consistency. Tying your worth to your ability will make you a slave to the world and your self-esteem. Your definitions of self will fluctuate and be contingent on factors you don't even have control over. For example, you may work your ass off to make partner at your law firm, and if for whatever reason you do not make partner, you may believe you are a bad lawyer = bad provider for your family = bad father, husband, and ultimately = less of a man. To come out of this, you will either work harder, putting more pressure on the "win", or cope in unhealthy ways.

This is the dangerous loop of tying who you are to what you can do. If we internalize this definition of manhood, then we believe that if we are bad at something, we are worthless, and that if we are good at something, we are worth more. Both beliefs are false. They are labels. We have been programmed this way. From our early days, we were praised for making the team, getting the girl, how hard we hit the ball, how much weight we could lift, what college we got into. We were praised on the size of our paycheck, our office, the letters after our name, and what we drove. Our brains got permanently set on accomplishments, accomplishments, accomplishments. Rarely did we ever get praise for our character, our compassion, or our capacity to love.

Your value lives in your character and capacity. Your heart and your story.

Your worth has nothing to do with what you can do. Your drive, passion, and ambition are all great gifts. Your athletic ability, your voice, your ability to lead, create, and change the world are imperative to your journey as a man. *But they do not determine your worth.* Your true value is what you bring to the table as a human being. This means not what you do but rather who you are.

The measure of a man is his inner self. It's who you are that will get you through the rough patches of life, never what you've done or built.

#39
Don't Punch Clocks

"**F**uck purpose. Let me build my empire. There is no such thing as what you were meant to do. This is America. You can do anything you want. It's time to get mine."

Like everyone else (and especially those living in New York and LA), that was my mind-set. I needed to sell scripts so I could get my house in the hills and have the matching Porsche/Rover combo in my horseshoe-shaped driveway. That was my "purpose". To buy things . . . so I could be happy.

I sat in coffee shops desperately pounding keys. Day after day, week after week, month after month, year after year. I became a fucking zombie chasing a commercial. Spent zero time on anything except framing this movie poster I had in my head starring John Empty Kim.

It wasn't until the universe ripped that poster in half by pulling my life rug out from under me that I discovered the actual importance of the word "purpose". You know the story. I got a divorce, changed careers from screenwriter to therapist, and started working at a nonprofit helping teenagers with their addictions. Purpose didn't hit me over the head. It's not like I suddenly woke up every morning with a heart boner to help kids. I dreaded it. Because I was a kid myself. I was still holding on to me, myself, and I. It's not like I didn't work hard as a screenwriter. I worked my ass off, wrote like a fucking maniac. But eventually, it lacked soul. I was writing to chase something instead of writing from passion. I was on autopilot, so the universe threw me into nonprofit and paired me up with hundreds of other lost souls just like me. At the time I felt like I was stepping down, giving up. But I was actually stepping up. Lives were at risk. And by helping other souls, I saved mine. I accepted my path. I rolled up my fucking sleeves and said, "Okay, let's do this." I stopped making it about me for the first time in my life. And the funny thing about the universe is that when you stop making it about you, the universe will make it happen for you.

I didn't find purpose like a ten-dollar bill on the street. It was a very slow burn. *For anyone who tells you to find your purpose, tell them to fuck off, because sometimes that shit needs to find you.* That was my case. I didn't wake up one day saying I was going to help people. No, I woke up one day and told myself I wanted to be honest with myself. I followed my new promise to myself with my actions, and slowly my life lined up and a vague sense of purpose started to appear. It would take years for me to really see what my purpose was. But it doesn't come to you just because you follow what you're passionate about. *Passion doesn't always equal purpose.* Your purpose is greater than you and what you want to do sometimes. It comes to you when you become self-aware, really start to know yourself. And that shit takes time. Then you discover your gifts as a being, and purpose grows at the intersection of who you are and what you can do (gifts/passion).

> **IF YOU CAN'T FIND SOMETHING TO LIVE FOR, YOU BEST FIND SOMETHING TO DIE FOR.**
>
> **– TUPAC**

Imagine a tyre. A flat one. Spinning in mud. As you decide to become self-aware and look inward, the tyre begins to inflate. When you begin to execute change by incorporating your revelations into action, exploring your thoughts and behavior, breaking unhealthy patterns, and walking in this new version of yourself, knobbies begin to appear on the tyre. This gives the tyre traction, which causes movement. The tyre is no longer spinning. You are now moving . . .

Then once you are out of the mud, sooner or later there will be more rough terrain. This rough terrain is called life, and it doesn't end until you end. It comes in the form of relationships, breakups, events, triggers, losing jobs, friends, restarting your life, situations you can control and some you cannot. You will get stuck many more times. But if through your growth process you discover your purpose, those knobbies turn into giant titanium claws. No matter what terrain or mountain lies ahead, your knowing who you are (which is constantly changing) plus what you are meant to do in this life will get you up, over, and through.

Knowing your purpose is the ultimate traction in life. It is a Sherman tank. It will always be the vine that pulls you out, no matter how thick the quicksand. Because your purpose is greater than you. It's greater than your marriage, kids, and career. Your purpose is your North Star, and you must follow it like a dog finding its way home.

Purpose is not a singular path that leads to a giant bell you must ring. You can have many purposes. They can change as you change, and they most likely will because you will. Today, I believe my purpose is to create a dialogue about living a better life and to help people help people (train life coaches). Tomorrow, who knows?

But it all starts with self-awareness, looking inward to truly see yourself, before you can start reaching for external goals. Every man must ask himself two questions: First, *Where am I going?* And second, *Who's coming with me?* If he reverses the order, he will be going alone.

#40
Do Be Aware
of Your Energy

Only a few years ago, I associated the word "energy" with solar power, batteries, electric cars, and the amount of human fuel I had for the day.

Today, energy is one of the first words that come to mind when I think of self-awareness, relationships, and, well, being a successful man.

We all know someone who enters a room and sucks the living shit out of your energy. (And if you don't, it might be you.) Because there's always that one person—the one who is angry, complainy, and always negative no matter what. He never sees the glass as half full, and you can smell the thick dark cloud around him. Well, I was that guy and completely oblivious of it. I was just being me. I wasn't happy. So I figured I'd wear it on my sleeve, disguised as a cynical, miserable fuck. If I covered it up, I would be being fake, right? Wrong. It wasn't until I was on the receiving end that I learned about the importance of being aware of your energy.

He was a friend I was writing a screenplay with, so we got together every day for hours on end. All he would do was tell me about his problems, talk shit about other people, and complain about everything from his coffee to his roommate. I wasn't his writing partner, I was his therapist. The problem was, he wasn't paying me. It got so bad I didn't want to be around him anymore. Ever. It wasn't his intention, but holy fuck, he brought me down with him every . . .

single . . . day. He hijacked the little positive energy that I did have at the time. I felt powerless and wanted to stay away from him, but I couldn't because we were writing partners. I suddenly saw him as a child. A boy.

One day on my way home from another shitty writing session I held the mirror up to myself, thought about all the relationships I had been in, and how irresponsible I was with my own energy. I was the same as this guy. I drained the people around me. Hijacked their positivity. In more than one of my relationships I remember them saying, *"John, I don't think you're happy."* And I remember how defensive I was. *"What do you mean I'm not happy? I laugh and joke around all the time. What are you talking about?"* Looking back on those relationships, it was clear: I wasn't aware of my energy. Sarcasm doesn't mean you're happy, and it sure as hell doesn't put out good energy into the world. I realized how hard that must have been to be around day after day, especially if we were living together. It's emotional abuse that you can't escape. It's poison for the other person. And it makes me sad to think about it now. Embarrassed. I felt like a child. And no wonder, because if you're not aware and responsible for your own energy, you are a child. It's like walking around with shit in your pants. It's not just annoying. It's offensive. It stinks up people's space, their day, their life.

At the risk of sounding too much like I've just walked off the playa at Burning Man, I'll just say it: we are all energy.

We literally emit energy that's produced by our thoughts and feelings. If we're constantly thinking and feeling negative feelings, like anger, hate, resentment, jealousy, etc., we emit negative energy. If we are thinking and feeling positive feelings, like love, gratitude, joy, etc., we emit positive energy. That's it. No need to go deeper.

As men, it's not just our words and actions we must take responsibility for. It is also our energy.

No, you can't see this process. And since we are such logical creatures, it may be difficult for you to put much weight on it. We need proof. Okay, here it is: How do you feel when you're riding shotgun with someone who has road rage? Holy shit. It's exhausting, right? His rage is activating your fight-or-flight. You're hitting your foot on an imaginary brake. He's vomiting negative energy—in this case, anger—and you're directly absorbing it. By the time you guys get to your destination, you are completely drained.

On the flip side, have you been around someone who is always calm and positive? Never complains or talks shit. Always tries to see the good in people and situations. How do you feel around that person? He's like water. You gravitate toward him. You look forward to seeing him. As you leave him, checking yourself and your own energy, you realize that actually, maybe being positive is a choice.

What does energy have to do with success? Well, our definitions of manhood often tell us that the alpha male, the one beating his chest and intimidating others, is the natural leader, the chief. But think about these two examples: the maniac screaming at the wheel, and the optimist who is easy breezy and at peace. Ask yourself: Who would you follow as a leader?

As men, at home, at work, in the world, it's not just our words and actions we must take responsibility for. It is also our energy. People can feel that shit. Kids can feel that shit even more. And it affects them. It's subtle trauma. They grow up walking on eggshells. Or being unaware of their own negative energy because they see it as normal. When it comes to your intimate relationship, recognize that it is extremely difficult to be intimate with someone who is always emitting negativity.

Stop taking people hostage with your negativity. Stop stripping them of their desire to live a good, positive life.

Today I make a daily effort to be aware of my energy and responsible for it. If I'm in a bad place or feeling down or negative, I make sure I don't put it on others. I mean, if I'm sitting down with a friend and we're talking about life, sure I can and should be real with them and tell them where I'm at. But I do it with consent. I do it with awareness. It's not forced. I am no longer a walking tornado. No, you shouldn't hold things in. Yes, you should vent. Especially men. But there is a time and place: Therapy rooms. The gym. When you're running alone. Not at other people, especially if you care about them.

#41
Do Make Your Bed

Why fix something that's just going to get messed up ten hours later? Besides, who's going to see it? Right? Also, that ten extra minutes can go toward an apple fritter on the way to work. But here's the truth: your potential is at stake. Let me explain.

As I've said before, I never had chores growing up. My mom did everything. She cleaned my room, did my laundry, and made my bed. It's embarrassing to admit, but it's true. So you can imagine that when I got married and moved in with my wife, she thought I was a child. She thought I was lazy. Rightfully so. But it wasn't that I was lazy. I just wasn't used to it. My wife came from the other side of the spectrum. She grew up with room inspections and believed that nothing is worth doing unless you do it right. This created conflict, which, on the surface, seemed like it was just a simple difference in morning routines. After our divorce, though, I realized how important it is to make your bed every morning. Not just because you're an adult and you should make your fucking bed. This isn't just about not being messy or upsetting your partner. It is about taking responsibility for your space and respecting yourself (and whoever else sleeps in your bed).

On the surface, making your bed shows that you are clean, responsible, and a functioning adult. But on a deeper, subconscious level, you are announcing to your partner, but more importantly to yourself, that you are going somewhere. Literally. You are now leaving your nest to do something in the world. You have direction, a dream, fire in your belly. There's something about making your bed in the morning. It's a respect thing. A character thing. A rite-of-passage thing. It's like a firm handshake. It says everything about you. It means you are certain, fearless, and determined. It means you respect yourself. All this just from making your bed?

Yes. The subconscious message is powerful. You are telling yourself you have an intention, a direction. You are saying you're going to go out and make something of yourself today. It's like the peeing-in-the-shower thing. It's not just about making your bed. It's about the announcement. To yourself and the world.

You are announcing to your partner, but more importantly to yourself, that you are going somewhere.

And of course, it's also about not being a slob. Because that's not really attractive, and if you do it long enough, your partner will start to see you differently. As a boy instead of a man. There will be hairline cracks in the chemistry. Not making your bed could hurt you in the bedroom, if you know what I mean. If you don't make your bed, the only thing you'll be doing there is sleeping on it.

Today, it doesn't matter if I'm single or in a relationship. I can't leave my bedroom unless I make my bed. And look, I'll be honest. I don't make it like there's going to be a military inspection or how housekeeping does it at fancy hotels. I just make sure it doesn't look slept in. Because I'm not sleeping. Because I am awake. Because I'm going to get some shit done today. Because today is not yesterday.

It's a new day. A new start. And making my bed is me saying that in action first thing in the morning.

#42
Do Fail, Often

failed as a screenwriter. I had a failed marriage. I had failed friendships. I had many failed businesses. I failed at CrossFit competitions. I've had so many failed attempts to use the internet in different ways to help people. I've failed at video courses. I've failed at programs. I've failed to hold on to nine-to-five jobs. I've failed at speaking.

If I was to count how many times I have "failed", it would be in the double digits for sure. But were they really failures, or were they soil for success to grow? If I look at all the things I have succeeded at, they could not have come if I hadn't had my failures. The "failures" created learning and ideas. For example, my screenwriting career. You can say I failed at that. But if I hadn't, I would never have become a therapist, found a sense of purpose, and you would not be reading this book right now. You can also say I "failed" at my marriage, but that led me down a path of self-discovery and helping others with their relationships and marriages. Those are just the big ones. I've failed at many businesses and attempts at multiple ideas. The "failures" were seeds planted that would later bear fruit. Of course, I didn't know that at the time. They felt fucking horrible. Every time I failed at something, I wanted to quit. It doesn't matter if I failed at lifting a certain weight or if I lost a hundred grand on a "crazy John Kim" idea that eventually fell flat. It was so hard to not tie my worth and

FAILURE IS A BADGE OF HONOUR.

– CHARLIE KAUFMAN

ability to outcomes. But I've learned that the only way to build something is to fail. There is no other way. It doesn't matter what you're building—a tree house or an empire. I don't know anyone who has built something amazing from just one attempt. Usually it takes many, many failures. So I've learned to fail, and fail often. I am no longer afraid to fail. I actually lean into it, knowing what's on the other side.

To fail is to build.

If you don't fail, you won't build anything. And men are meant to build things. (Actually, all people are.) There is growth in the process of creating, carving, assembling parts to execute a vision. It gives you a sense of purpose and accomplishment. When I was a kid, I would lock myself in a room and build with my Legos for hours on end. I would lose track of time. I would forget to eat. I remember how alive I felt. Then I grew up and life happened, and I forgot what building felt like. Because I was busy chasing instead of building (attracting). Until I went through my rebirth and started building something again. This time, me.

I've learned that building creates a greater sense of self. But the value is not in what you have built or are building. It's in the struggle—sweat, passion, persistence, courage, attitude, vision, dreams, and of course the lessons from the failures. And that's the part that makes men. Men who build know what it means to invest themselves and their beliefs in something. They have calluses, not only on their hands but on their determination. Building something creates a life that is greater than you.

#43
Do Have
a Firm Handshake

There are two types of men. Men who look you in the eye and shake your hand firmly, and men who look down at their shoes and hand you a dead fish. The first is the type of man who makes decisions. He is confident. He knows who he is. You can trust him. He is honorable. The second is filled with ambivalence. He's indecisive and unsure of himself. He is slippery and avoidant. He doesn't know where to go on dates or what to order on the menu; he is selfish in bed and runs funny. All this from a handshake? Yes. A man's handshake says everything about him.

Our handshake reflects our perception of self. A weak grip and scrambling eyes stem from ambivalence and insecurity. We believe we are not enough, less than. This false belief causes us to look for shortcuts and avoid confrontations. It's a way of hiding. We are afraid. On the other hand, a firm handshake stems from certainty, a belief that we are enough. A strong grip with eye contact and a confident smile says, *I am valuable, I am worthy, and I am here. It's a pleasure to meet you.*

Our handshake reflects
our perception of self.

Use shaking someone's hand as an exercise to build self-confidence and be the kind of person you strive to be.

THE EXTRAS

(how you show up)

If your eyes are the windows to your soul, your handshake is the doorway to your beliefs about self and the ripple you want to send out into the world. But there are other indicators. Be aware of the following:

- **Your clothes**

  It doesn't matter what your style is; just make sure your clothes fit. Unless you're eight, don't look like a walking pillow. Or like you shop at babyGap. Wear clothes that actually fit your body type.

- **Your shoes**

  It doesn't matter if you own only one pair of sneakers. Just make sure they are not lopsided, worn down to the sole, or half laced, and don't have holes in them. Wear clean shoes. Women notice your shoes more than anything else you wear.

- **Your social media photos**

  There's nothing wrong with a filtered photo once in a while that makes you look like you should adorn the cover of *GQ* or a fitness magazine, but don't turn your camera into a carnival mirror. Take some real pictures that actually look like you. Or you're just screaming, *I don't like myself.*

- **Your posts**

  It doesn't matter how many people are following you. Your social media posts are an extension of you. Just be aware of that and post according to what's honest to you, your passions, values, ideas, humor—whatever. But make sure they line up with who you are and who you want to be.

- **Your bed**
Don't just make sure it's made. Make sure they're not the same sheets you've had since college. Get some real fucking sheets. A whole set that goes together. It's called bedding.

- **Your bathroom**
Keep that shit clean. No one expects to eat off the floor, but clean up all the hairs after you shave, and use bleach! More on all that later.

The next time you shake someone's hand, grip it with authority. Remind yourself what the behavior means, the message it sends, not only to the other person, but, more importantly, to yourself. You matter. You're alive. You affect others. This is part of growing up: believing that you are more than a cardboard cutout. And a firm handshake says that louder than words. *Boys exist. Men punctuate.* Even if you doubt yourself, make sure your handshake doesn't say that. By changing behavior, beliefs can also change. See it as an opportunity for growth. Introduce yourself to the world.

#44
Do Enter Rooms
Like You Own Them

I had the opportunity to see a silverback gorilla a few years ago when I took the teenagers I was treating in a residential treatment center to the zoo. He was the most massive, powerful, and intimidating animal I've ever seen in my life. His arms were like tree trunks. When he ran toward you, you could literally feel the ground thunder. But it wasn't the six hundred pounds of muscle that were shit-your-pants frightening. There are bears, elephants, lions, and other animals just as massive. It was his stance, his posture, his calm but confident energy, and the certainty in his eyes communicating three words: *I am here.*

In CrossFit, when you're doing a dead lift, the coaches scream, "Gorilla chest!" This means push your chest out. Do not round your back or you will lose it. This posture prevents injury, but it also creates power. You are positioning yourself to stand upright, which produces belief. Chest out and up. Your form acts as a sealant that keeps the energy from leaking. You can feel it as it enters your body, in your grip, in the weight of your heels. It's this anchor that allows you to lift more weight than you've ever imagined.

Just like your handshake, your posture and the way you walk into rooms are a direct reflection of what you think about yourself. Do you slip into a room slouched and invisible? Or do you enter with certainty? You will know by people's reactions. Either they will act as though you are wallpaper, or they will notice you and instinctively step aside. There is power in posture and the way you carry your body. That being said, know that there is a difference between posture and posturing. One stems from certainty. The other from ego, from approval-seeking insecurity. If you want to be noticed for what you lack, opt for posturing. If you want to be noticed for who you are, walk with a gorilla chest.

Your posture and the way you walk into rooms are a direct reflection of what you think about yourself.

It doesn't matter if you don't believe in yourself or if you have low self-esteem. Not everyone can honestly walk into a room like they own it. The point is that you try. That's what makes you a man. Your desire and courage to be visible. If you don't believe you exist, no one else will either.

#45
Do Believe in Yourself

I know this sounds clichéd, but it all starts and ends here. You have to believe in yourself, because when you start to believe in yourself, you start to believe in your story, and when you start to believe in your story, your path reveals itself. And you become fearless, because it's not about you anymore.

So believing in yourself isn't about you. It's about all you're meant to do. You have to believe in yourself. If not for you, then for the rest of us. So we can experience your gifts.

It doesn't matter how you get there. Mantras, meditation, setting yourself up for new, challenging, and different experiences—whatever works for you. For me, it was a very slow burn that took nearly a decade, and I still struggle with it daily.

Knowing your value, ability, and purpose is a process. For some it takes a lifetime, but you cannot be on that journey until you first believe in yourself. That being said, there are going to be days when you don't believe in yourself. There are going to be days when you feel like you were not meant to change anything. That is okay. I feel that way often. That is part of the process.

Believing in yourself is not a constant. It is a mind-set, and it takes time, effort, and work. It's less about the trudge and more about the choice to be on that path. But there is a tipping point.

PUTTING IT INTO PRACTICE:
how to start
believing in yourself today

Reworth yourself

When you believe you're worth something, the universe moves. I believe this with every fiber of my being. The internal shift that happens when you are convinced of your value and unique gifts changes every . . . single . . . thing. Your belief produces a be-ing that attracts people and opportunities, setting you up for new experiences that will continue to shift your thinking instead of limiting you with mental ceilings and false beliefs.

Instead of sucking energy and getting caught in vicious negative thought patterns that dilute your being, strip your soul, and smash your dreams, you begin to generate energy that punctures space and grabs stars.

Everything ends or begins with your beliefs. What you believe will determine where you will go. Throughout your life, you've read and seen what is possible. People can pretty much do anything. But you don't believe that's possible for you. Good things happen only to others. But that's only because you haven't experienced them, and you haven't experienced them because you don't believe you can, and you maybe don't believe you can because you don't believe you have worth. If you don't believe you have value, you'll never live a meaningful life. You will merely exist. So the question is, How do you believe you're worth more?

Worth is not something you believe. It's something you build. Read that sentence again, because most people think they either believe or they don't. They don't understand that they can build their worth. Or in my words, reworth themselves. We do this by creating new experiences → shifts beliefs → more new experiences → new beliefs.

Most of us have been cut at the knees at one time or another, which has dropped our value. Or at least we believe that. We had to start over. We went through some sort of internal collapse. We lost businesses, marriages, friendships, and we tie all that to our worth, so the external events that happen in our lives fuck up our internal beliefs about ourselves.

And it's going to happen again. That's what life is about. Obstacles and challenges. Constantly coming at us like waves in the ocean. But we can learn how to ride them instead of drowning in them. And sometimes, we catch the wave. Other times, we fall. But if we keep believing we have value, we will never drown. And I say "keep believing" because believing you have worth is a process. It's not just a decision or a one-time thing. We have to constantly reworth ourselves. For me, it's a way of living.

Let's break it down.

The first step is connection.

I always tell people that growth is sometimes more about a reunion than anything else. A reunion to self, parts of you that you stuffed into a hope chest for when life happened, when you had to "grow up". Most of us live disconnected with ourselves. We live in a chasing state and exchange who we truly are for approval and validation. To fit in. To impress others. To feel valuable. But that's not internal value. That's an external value. Internal worth is not contingent on what others think of you. Internal value hangs on what you think about yourself.

Connect to yourself

The call to action here is to allow yourself to be truly and uniquely you. It's that simple. Not easy, but also not complicated. And by doing so, you will start connecting with yourself. Get comfortable with yourself. Like yourself. Trust yourself. I talk a lot about our Solid (true) Self and our Pseudo (false) Self. Connecting to you means to pull from your Solid, daily. As much as you can, because depending on your environment and who you're around, your tug will fluctuate. At times, it will be easy. And at times, it will feel impossible. So you practice it as if it's a daily exercise, and the more you do it, the easier it becomes to pull from your Solid Self.

This means keeping promises you made to yourself. This means disengaging from toxic relationships that puncture your self-worth. This means getting out of shitty jobs that gray you out. This means standing on your truth at the risk of pushback from people you care about and seek approval from. This means being okay with not being okay. Until you are okay. And realizing your world did not collapse. People still love you.

The way you connect to yourself is different for everyone. But I believe it takes a daily ritual. A practice. Like meditation. Like fitness. Like breakfast. Because we are always connecting and disconnecting with ourselves, even if it's subtle. The more connected we are to our true selves, the more worth we will build.

Here are some of the things I do.

Put as much distance as you can between you and your thoughts. Our thinking can drown us pretty fast. The way you do it is up to you. Most people meditate and practice mindfulness. Focus on breath. Allow thoughts to come and go without attaching to them. Be as present as you can. Again, this is a daily practice. As you create this distance, you create soil, a rich soil that will ground you. And as you ground yourself, you can start to really be aware of how you feel and where things are coming from. You can separate what's yours and your truth from what's not. Then you can start connecting and honoring you. Give yourself permission to be. This may be uncomfortable for many, since we judge ourselves constantly. Another way to connect to you is through an activity. For example, yoga. Art. Music. Cooking. For me, it's fitness and riding motorcycles. Something you enjoy doing that puts you into a flow state where you lose track of time because you're so immersed in the activity. Athletes tap into this state often. This process allows you to connect to you. You become very potent in this state. It doesn't matter what the activity is. As long as it's honest to you and you enjoy it fully. This is why I keep saying, "Seek nectar." Fill your day with as much of this as possible so you are experiencing a lot of flow. It's really hard to worry and think about the future when you are in flow. Also, it doesn't have to be only leisure activities. You can tap into flow at work, as long as you enjoy what you do. You can hit flow states while doing anything creative.

Here's another way to connect to yourself. Fulfill your needs. We all have basic needs we need to fulfill. Because of life, we forget to fulfill them, and when we don't, we can start to feel disconnected from ourselves. Here are a few basic types of needs.

Emotional need
Your need to express yourself. To be heard.

Creative need
Your need to be creative. Use your right brain.

Sexual need
Your need to feel sexy. We are sexual beings.

Physical need
Your need to move. To connect with your body.

Intellectual need
Your need to feed your brain. If you don't feed it, you won't grow.

Spiritual need
Your need to feel connected to something greater than yourself. We are spiritual beings.

Passion/purpose need
Your need to feel you are on this planet for a reason. Because you are. How are you fulfilling these needs? Not once but daily. Fulfilling these needs creates bridges to yourself.

Get curious

Get very curious. About everything. Especially who you're becoming and what you can do. What's happening around you and why. The role the people in your life are supposed to play, the events that happen and what you're supposed to learn from them. How many people you can impact. Get curious about new definitions and what new experiences would feel like. Get super-curious. Because there is power in curiosity. It squashes judgment. Judgment keeps you narrow and stunted. Curiosity expands you. This expanding is a form of connecting to yourself.

Accept your story

So many of us want to rip out chapters. Every time we try to erase what has happened, we line our story with shame and guilt. Yes, a lot of bad has a happened. I'm a therapist. I've heard some crazy shit. We all have our stories. Many of us shouldn't even be alive. But we are, which just makes our stories more beautiful. I know it may not feel like it, but all parts of your story are important and meaningful. The events in our lives are like dominos. They need to happen in order to keep our stories moving forward and give our purpose a punch.

It's extremely difficult to accept what's happening when you're in the trenches. So you have to trust. You do that by looking back and connecting dots. You have to make sense of your story. Realize why things happened the way they did.

Know this: Every amazing story has an inciting incident, some event that throws our hero into the unknown. Every amazing story has turning points and act breaks and things we didn't see coming. The protagonist is faced with obstacles and challenges in order for her to enter her journey and come back to the village changed. So she could share her story with others. Without these things, there is no story. This is not just in books and movies. This is true for our lives as well. As you face hardships and slay your dragons, you become. You evolve. You find your cape.

Serve

Stop making it about you. Our value isn't just about connecting to ourselves. It's about connecting to others and the world. We are all connected in that way. When we use too many "I"s in our sentences, we start to disconnect from ourselves, and whenever we disconnect, we lose worth.

We all have unique gifts. To serve means to discover those gifts, hone them, and share them with the world. To throw your stone. As far as you can. That is your job. Your responsibility as a human being on this planet. The process of doing that creates value in you.

Reworth yourself by connecting to yourself, getting curious about what's possible, accepting your story, and sharing your gifts with the world by serving.

Then the universe will move for you.

You will start to appear.

We don't believe in ourselves due to the false beliefs we live with. These false beliefs run deep since they are tied to our story, the shit we went through, and how we were treated or raised. As we start to dissolve these false beliefs, we start to believe more and more in ourselves and what's possible. *There's nothing more convincing than a new experience. That's where new beliefs live.*

So to start dissolving your false beliefs, you have to start giving yourself new experiences. Here are three tips.

1. RUN FASTER THAN FEAR.

Fear is always the first wall. We are all afraid, mostly of failure. Use fear as emotional color dye so you know what you need to start leaning into. Put the cart before the horse, and pull the trigger on things before fear sets in. Sometimes, when we plan too much, we allow ourselves to become afraid. According to TV host and motivational author Mel Robbins, we have five seconds after our raw urge and instinct to do something before fear leaks in and prevents us. Take the first step before those five seconds are up.

2. FEEL IT.

You doubt because you haven't had the experience. You don't know that possibility exists. Visualize that experience. Don't only see it, but feel it in your bones as if it has already happened and you're replaying a memory. Visualize often, and get obsessed with it until you do everything you can to make it a reality. Attract that shit.

3. GET CURIOUS ABOUT WHAT YOU CAN DO.

Instead of feeding what you can't do, start getting very curious about what you can. There is enormous power in curiosity. You only have this life this way. You may come back a tree. Take advantage of your opportunity to explore and taste everything this life has to offer. Start living out your *what ifs*.

There is a day when you will wake up and believe in yourself more often than not. You will realize that your beliefs have shifted. That you can recover from a shattered heart. That you can push your body further than you think. That you can find joy in moments. That you don't have to be concerned with what others think. That someone can like you. That you can love again. That you can write a book. That you were meant to impact the world in some way.

As a man, your job is to find out how you're going to do it. There is no other way to look at life.

COMMUNICATION

Ah, communication. We communicate pretty well in meetings and when we're training with our boys (guy friends) at the gym. But when it comes to the most basic forms—bickering with our girlfriends, raging at the driver who just cut us off, expressing to a friend that our feelings were hurt—we're a mess.

Communication problems are the foundation of the issues I see most in my practice. But I'm happy to say that the solutions are so incredibly easy, you'll find communication to be a nonissue if you take a few simple steps.

COMMUNICATION,
in a shot glass:

Men have the ability to say no. Men put their phone down.
Men don't walk away during a fight. Men tip well. Men
don't argue. Men express their feelings. Men don't send
dick pics.

#46
Do Say No Often

This is something I still struggle with today. It's really difficult for me to say no, especially if you're a friend. Or a girlfriend. Or a family member. Or a perfect stranger. You want to work out even though it's my rest day? You need a ride to the airport even though I'm busy? You need help moving even though I would rather push needles into my eyes? You want to sit down and talk about you for an hour even though we just did that last weekend? Sure. Yes. Yes. Yes. I can say it's because I'm a therapist and I'm supposed to help people. But the truth is, I still struggle with wanting people to like me. I want to feel important. Valued. But at what expense?

A yes-man is constantly focused on pleasing others, even when it goes against his own truth. The fear of being unwanted or rejected overrides his opinions, perspective, and stance. He is a placater, an enabler, and ultimately a loner. The very behaviors that are meant to keep him on everyone's good side are the things that alienate him from them.

At work, the inability to say no turns you into a robot. You become a product; you're dispensable. If you can't say no in friendships, you become the designated driver, a therapist who doesn't get paid, and possibly a bank. You will be the first one they call if they need something, but the one they "forgot" to call when there's a party.

When you don't have the ability to say no in intimate relationships, you are creating an unsafe space. If you can't speak your truth—not for the sake of winning, but because it is your honest truth—she won't trust you. She needs to know that you can say no. Because it means you have a spine. It means you have opinions. It means you have something to stand for. But more importantly, it means you have courage. This means she has someone to lean on.

It's only in saying no that change can occur, respect can be earned, and a difference can be made. A truthful no opens eyes as well as doors. It also gives greater weight to the things you say yes to. Define your friendships instead of allowing them to define you. Get in the picture instead of holding the camera. *Say no and see who sticks around.* The ones who do are friends; the ones who don't aren't. If no one sticks around, you've been saying yes way too long.

A truthful no opens eyes as well as doors.

Getting over your fear of saying no and finally standing on your truth unleashes your potential to do the things you're passionate about and lets you be your greatest self as a boyfriend, husband, boss, employee, father, brother, son, and leader. It's not just about you and your fears. It's bigger than you. It's about the dent you want to make in this world.

#47
Do Try to Understand Before Trying to Be Understood

I was always the black sheep. I didn't do well in school. I forgot things. My mind was always elsewhere. I started way too many projects that I didn't finish. I was a dreamer. I rambled often. People never took me seriously. *Oh, that's just John being John.* I was a clown. My parents always worried about me. I was all over the place. Eventually people stopped listening to me. I often felt alone and/or misunderstood.

So as an adult, I made sure people understood me. Literally. I would be loud and aggressive to get my point or idea across. I didn't care what they had to say. I just cared about getting my opinion, thoughts, words in. Because it was tied to my worth. I didn't want to be misunderstood anymore. I wanted to matter. And the more important the person was to me, the more I did this. It turns out this doesn't work well in relationships. It's not a great way of communicating, and communication is the most important tool when building a relationship. Instead of using a power tool, I was building a relationship with a popsicle stick.

Do people often tell you to stop being defensive? Does your girlfriend or your mom ever tell you not to raise your voice during a fight? You wouldn't believe how many men struggle to communicate their position effectively in simple conversations, let alone in arguments or at important meetings. It is one of the things I hear most in my sessions with men. They often feel like they leave situations without being heard, so they overcompensate and then wonder, *Was I rude? Did I talk over people? What did the other person even say?* They leave conversations remembering only what they offered, and nothing the other person/people contributed. *Here's the trick: make understanding the priority, and being understood will follow.*

Imagine for a second if everyone tried to *understand* before trying to be understood. We enter most conversations trying to be understood first, and understand second. If both parties entered the conversation trying to understand, people would be less defensive. They'd really be hearing each other. Communicating. We might still disagree, but we would no longer be holding up shields, defending our position. We have let go of our tug-of-war rope. After understanding the other person, we can then express our opinion and how we feel, clearly and confidently. Since they feel understood, chances are they will do their best to understand us. This dynamic turns a crowbar into glue. It makes people feel closer.

> IT TAKES A GREAT
> MAN TO BE A
> GOOD LISTENER.
>
> – CALVIN
> COOLIDGE

We often argue when we don't feel heard. If you focus on understanding the person on the other end of the conversation above anything else, they will feel heard. And if you're thinking *Why can't they understand me first?* why not teach them how by being the example? Make them feel heard. And they will reciprocate.

Do you know how many fights could be prevented if people just practiced this one technique? How many marriages could be saved? How many people could learn, grow, and understand each other better? When we feel heard, we feel safe. When we feel safe, we can agree to disagree and it's okay. We can express ourselves and our point of view, and there won't be strong pushback or defensiveness. This becomes a safe space, groundwork for healthy communication and, ultimately, connection.

#48
Don't Walk Away During a Fight

The heated man who storms out of the room. We've seen this scene so many times. I grew up with this scene in person, in real life. All the men in my life had tempers and were highly reactive. None of them had the ability to stay in arguments and talk things out. Their voices grew strong and they left the room. This instantly cracks trust and creates an unsafe space.

There is absolutely no excuse to walk away from a fight. None. Zero. Zilch. The moment you walk away, you are not just leaving the conversation, you are leaving the relationship. What the other person is hearing is, *I don't care about you. I don't want to work on us. I cannot control my feelings. I'm done. I want out. Deal with it on your own. I don't love you.* Actions speak louder than words. Always. So if this is what you want to communicate, walk. But remember, she may not be there when you return.

No shocker here. I've had to learn this from experience. And I've come to discover that hanging up, slamming the door, or walking away during a fight sets the tone and the way fights will be handled in the future. You're saying it's okay to leave when you feel like it. If the other person also does the same thing, there is no communication and nothing will get resolved. What remains? Only resentment and people not feeling safe to talk about anything. Then you wonder why people walk on eggshells around you. You wonder why people hold things in. You wonder why there is drift and disconnect.

Safe and unsafe spaces.

The best way to break it down is into safe and unsafe spaces, caused by fair and unfair fighting.

Safe spaces. Empathy. Compassion. Calm. Communication. Responsiveness.

Unsafe spaces. Judgment. Explosiveness. Reactivity.

I know I've said this before and I'll say it a thousand more times. It's not about how many times we fight. It's about *how* we fight. Fight fair. Understand before trying to be understood. And don't walk away.

If there's one thing in relationships we really need to learn how to do more, it's to fight fair. It's a common theme I've found from helping thousands of couples with their rocky relationships. We don't fight fair. Imagine a boxing match where only one of the contestants can use a knife or a bat. Or leave when they feel like it. There are rules. Or it's war. Our fights are war, and we wonder why things aren't working out.

The more you are able to stay and fight fair, the more trust is built, and your relationship will be able to withstand ten times more than it did. But this isn't just with your partner. It's with everyone. Your friends. Your family. Your coworkers. And it's not just walking away. It can be shutting down emotionally. The inability to stay in the space where there's conflict is what I'm referring to. If things can't be worked out and both agree, then that's fair. It's time to separate. But just leaving unwarned is a reaction. Not a response. And like I mentioned earlier, boys react. Men respond.

Yes, women do it, too. I understand it's not a gender

thing. It's a human thing. Actually, it's a child/adult thing. It's the inability to control oneself.

Finally, it's not just about the relationship with others. It's about the relationship you have with you. You know what it feels like to leave something because you couldn't control yourself. We are hard on ourselves. We judge ourselves. We bash ourselves. Then we keep it inside and bottle it up. Eventually it comes out in ways we don't want it to. It's time to break that pattern. And if you can't do it for you, do it for all the boys growing up who are watching us as examples. Do it for the world.

#49
Do Express Your Fucking Feelings

My very first blog post ever, nearly a decade ago, was on Tumblr and was titled "My Fucking Feelings":

Today I am sad. I am sad that the world is shaking and people are dying. I am sad that I can't be a better son, brother, or friend. I am sad for the 14 teenagers I treat for substance abuse and the shitty cards they were dealt. I am sad I wasn't present in past relationships. I am sad there is hate in the world. I am sad that we live in a fatherless nation. I am sad because it's raining. I am sad that I pre-judge. I am sad that I can't apologize to some people. I am sad that I want material things. I am sad that my parents are aging. I am sad that I need attention. Today, I am sad.

I had no idea if anyone would read it. I had no idea it would be in a book one day. I just wrote my feelings, because I didn't feel like I had anything else. I felt like life took everything and it's all I had. So I posted my fucking feelings. And to be honest, what's important about this blog post isn't the content. I mean, I've written better blogs. Let's hope so! It was important because it was the first time I wrote my feelings down on paper. Ever. It was the first domino to many more blogs expressing myself. And that expression, that process, is what gave me a voice. Not just as a writer, but as a person. As a man.

Yes, it's a generalization you've heard a million times: Women are more emotional. Men are more logical. But there's truth to it or you wouldn't be rolling your eyes right now. As men we tend to hold things in. Bottle our feelings inside. Part of that is due to the generational transmission process. Our great-grandfathers passed down their actions and definitions of what a man looks like to our grandfathers,

---

How to express your fucking feelings.

Here are some great ways to start thinking about saying how you feel. You can start small—no need to go on a feeling bender all of a sudden.

1. **Sit with it.** First, you must be aware of your feelings. Most of us are so used to suppressing and deflecting our feelings that we are uncomfortable sitting with them. When we feel something uncomfortable, we instantly let logic take the steering wheel. We must break this pattern by paying attention to what we're feeling. By sitting with your feelings, you are acknowledging that they exist. Don't judge them. Just be aware that they are there. This only makes you human.

2. **Do a body scan.** At any moment in the day you can take one deep breath and tell yourself what you're feeling. Where do you feel the tension? Shoulders? Stomach? Are you worried about having dinner with your parents? Are you excited about a date? Are you sad? Are you overjoyed?

3. **Release through movement.** Maybe you don't like to journal or don't do it enough for it to be effective. If you can't sit down and write about your feelings every day, another way to release them is through movement. Yoga. Hiking. CrossFit. The movement doesn't matter. It's all about your intention. Notice your feelings as you are doing your preferred activity, and use movement to release them. Use the anger, frustration, sadness, jealousy—any feeling you are experiencing—as energy to move you. Then allow those feelings to move through you.

---

who passed down their actions and definitions to our fathers and so on. Part of their wiring has to do with the society/ world they lived in. It was a different time then. Therapy, wellness, and people like Brené Brown, who researches the power of vulnerability, were not around. There was no dialogue created to challenge men and their definitions.

So we grow up watching other men bottling up their emotions inside, then exploding when they can't handle it anymore. Or maybe they don't explode. They stay calm and just go into fix-it mode. Which is another way of coping. Running. Not facing your self. Whatever the case, we've watched men who are emotionally absent; we are not taught how to express ourselves. Like seeking nectar or enjoying our time alone, expressing our feelings becomes a muscle we just don't exercise.

Imagine watching a movie where the main character never went through an emotional journey. He fought battles and climbed mountains, but there was no inner character arc. The story would run flat. You wouldn't care or be invested in the protagonist. It would just be a visual ride. It's the same with all of us. In real life. If we don't express ourselves and what we're going through to the people we care about and the people who care about us—the people watching our movie—if we don't show the people we love our emotional character arc, our movie runs flat. Our story has little impact. Self-expression is not just about you. It's required for your story to be powerful and have an impact on others.

50
Do Put
Your Phone Down

I t all started with the pager. This little vibrating gizmo was more than a connection device: it made us feel important. Every time our hip vibrated, we saw our Bat-Signal in the sky. We felt wanted and needed. Some of us had two of them, one for business and one for personal use. People noticed them. We liked that people noticed them. It made us feel powerful.

Then came cell phones. They were big and expensive. It was a luxury to have one. It meant we had money or were in the process of making it. It gave us attention as well as a voice. People noticed them. We liked that people noticed them. It made us feel powerful.

Once cell phones became mainstream, it was less about how it made us feel and more about what we could do with it. Technology turned our Pseudo Self Solid. We weren't trying to sell anymore. Instead, we were bought.

Today, we can't function without these little devices. We are on them constantly. Work, home, car, gym, lunch, bathroom, and on dates. If we lose one of them or leave it at home, instant panic sets in. They keep us connected to the world. But the truth is, they keep us trapped in our own bubble. They allow us to hide. The next generation will have fewer social skills due to their cell phones. They will be the first generation where actually asking a woman out in person is *not* the normal way to do it.

Clearly, being on your smartphone when you're in the

presence of company is a rude ritual. Your mind is somewhere else. You are not giving the other person your undivided attention. But this is not just about being respectful to your company. It's about man versus machine. These devices are supposed to connect us, but they are actually pulling us apart.

I coached a couple once whose main issue was that the girlfriend was on her phone from the time she woke up to the time she went to bed. She never put it down. Meals. Movies. It didn't matter. Even during sex, she would stop and check it if she received a message or notification. She was a yoga influencer with a substantial following. Her argument was that it was her "job". But it wasn't just her job. It became her addiction. She was addicted to the dopamine she got from likes and follows. But on a deeper level, I believe it was a way to get back at her ex-boyfriend, who had been obsessed with video games years back and neglected her. They eventually broke up. It's sad to me that our devices, things that are designed to make the world easier and connect us, are becoming a catalyst for our disconnect and addictions.

Phones were not meant to replace communication. Instead of using them as a tool, we are using them as a crutch. We must put our phones down and look into eyes instead of screens. We must tame our machines. Own them before they own us. We must respect our kind. Or we will have no one to text.

#51
Do Be Physically Affectionate

After forty-four years, I have yet to see my father display any form of physical affection toward my mother. Let me rephrase that: He has tried to steal kisses as a joke or to get a reaction, primarily for the sake of entertaining his sons. But never a heart touch—a touching of hearts with other parts. (Yes, I did just say that. No, I will not apologize. . . But back to my dad.) No hugs, no kisses, no holding hands, not even a squeeze on the shoulder to remind my mom she is not alone in this world. Today, they sleep in separate bedrooms. Sometimes I wonder how I was created.

I understand we all have different love languages, but relationships are like cell phones. Without full bars, the connection is poor. With poor connection, people drift. Physical affection and touch are one way to keep those bars strong while you're hitting dry patches. Or while you're not. Do you avoid displaying physical affection because you're embarrassed? If that's the case, you're with the wrong person or you seek too much approval. No? That's not it? Oh, you're just not a touchy-feely person? And where do you think you learned that from? This behavior is a virus that will be passed down through the generations. Unless someone stops it. Break the cycle. Something as simple as a hand on a shoulder or a palm on a back validates, confirms, and assures that you are present, investing in this relationship.

#52
Don't Drive Like
a Dick

My best friend egged me on in the next lane. That's why I did it, which is no excuse, but I was a boy then. Within five seconds, I surpassed the freeway speed limit in my brand-new Mazda RX-7 twin turbo. I think I was going ninety-five when my girlfriend screamed, "Stop!" But I ignored her. I had something to prove. I wanted to win. Looking back, I don't remember who won the race. All I remember is the terror etched in my girlfriend's face as tears streamed down her cheeks.

I understand you like driving fast. I get the adrenaline rush. But on a deeper level, sometimes we use our driving to let out steam and/or be someone we can't be in our "real" life. For example, if you're not assertive or struggle with standing up for yourself, you may overcompensate by being aggressive and taking no shit when you're behind the wheel. We feel powerful and fearless in our cars because we are protected by sheet metal. We are anonymous. We can hide. We can be someone else. This is why road rage is so common. In our cars, we allow ourselves to go from Bruce Banner to the Incredible Hulk. Of course, at work and home there are consequences, so we don't allow that to happen there.

What if it's not about overcompensation? What if you are an enthusiast? What if you have a sports car and want to drive it like it's supposed to be driven? Well then, take it to the track.

This was a tough one for me. I've gone off-roading on

people's private lawns to impress the passenger in my truck. I've stopped on railroad tracks and then peeled out at the last second before a train comes. I've done doughnuts or driven in reverse for blocks on a dare. When you're in the driver's seat, it's easy to act like a dick. But flip the script. Have you been the passenger of someone who drives recklessly? Have you ridden shotgun while the driver screams and yells and cuts people off, pulls in front of someone and slams his brakes? How did it make you feel? It might have been fun when you were in high school, but most likely you were just going with the flow and didn't want to be the straight kid who doesn't like danger. You wanted to be cool, as I did. But as an adult, how does that experience make you feel about the driver? Does it change your opinion about him? I find it offensive. Rude. Annoying. Inconsiderate. I don't see him as a badass. I see him as a posturing idiot who can't control his rage. When you drive, you are communicating to the world. You are saying either that you are in control and value the safety of others. Or that you can't control yourself and don't give two shits about other people. You decide which message you want to share.

How to cure your road rage

Know that once you get into your vehicle, whether you have a passenger or not, you are putting lives at stake. This means you have a responsibility. It's not just about you and the rush you want to feel or the shit you won't take from others. It's about being a responsible human being. In other words, being an adult. Or in this case, a man.

Three tips to stop your road rage:

1. **Pretend it's your mom driving every other car.** I'm dead serious. You will be so much more forgiving. We get enraged because we think the other driver is being aggressive. And we take that aggression personally. But if we tell ourselves a different story, we won't take it so personally. Maybe they just don't know how to drive. Like our moms. And if your mom is a great driver, it's much easier to forgive her if she slips up and cuts you off.

2. **Feel sorry for them.** Not in a patronizing way. I mean, truly practice empathy. Know that their aggression is telling of where they're at in their lives and that that shit comes back around. Behavior ripples. So that rage is happening in other areas of their life. And it's making their life harder. It's something they are struggling with. Give them grace.

3. **Use their temper as a way to exercise yours.** If you challenge yourself to not allow someone else's state—in this case, rage—to affect yours, you are not allowing them to have power over you. You are power-filled instead of powerless. And that's something to be proud of. It means you've come a long way. If you fall into the trap and react with road rage, well, then you still have some work to do.

#53
Don't Debate
Everything

When I was married, I got into an argument with my wife once over tinted windows. We were sitting in her car. It was hot. She had very fair skin and was complaining about the sun damaging it when she drove. I told her she should tint her side window because it would block the damaging UV rays. She didn't believe that the tint protected her from the sun. I knew for a fact that it did. My brother worked in the automotive industry. I had scientific proof! So we argued, back and forth. Both of us not letting down. Eventually she gave up and broke down. She started crying. I sat there confused at how we went from a friendly argument about tinted windows to her sobbing. I didn't raise my voice. It was a very calm and logical argument. It wasn't until years later that I realized I wasn't making any effort to understand her. Instead, I wanted her to understand me. It wasn't about tinted windows. It was about someone feeling unheard, and therefore unsafe. And of course this was a pattern, since I wasn't aware of myself and my actions and how they impacted others. That's probably why she broke down. She had had enough. I wanted to win. I was a child.

Now, I'm not saying you shouldn't state your opinions or what's on your mind. It was completely okay for me to tell her what I knew about tinted windows. I'm talking about not letting it go and drilling it until someone finally gives up. That's not communication. That's retaliation. Self-expression means you state your opinion or how you feel, without retaliation.

Arguments are usually about two hurt people not being heard. Like my tinted window story, it's rarely about what they are arguing about. It's what's underneath. But instead of hearing each other and addressing the hurt, we get into a rat race to see who can win, pull out the most shit from the past, or just be right. This creates a wall. It pulls people away from each other instead of bringing them together. Wanting to be right. Wanting to win. All that is purely ego driven.

DO YOU WANT TO BE RIGHT OR DO YOU WANT TO BE HAPPY?

– DR. PHIL

A healthy argument is one person expressing herself and the other person accepting her expression and then vice versa. Yes, you can disagree. Yes, you can try to get the other person to see your side. But only for a limited period of time. *There's a point where a disagreement turns into an argument.* You know because you can feel it. Emotions get involved, and when emotions get involved, people are no longer hearing each other. We are too busy pulling on our tug-of-war rope. We instantly become opponents, competitors, enemies.

I used to argue about everything. There was always a but or should or "What about this?" after every sentence. I couldn't just take in someone's opinion or self-expression and be okay with it. Even if I went into it gently or slowly, at the end of the day I was still arguing. Arguing was a by-product, a direct reaction to my discomfort and insecurity. When someone doesn't believe what we believe, we feel uneasy. We feel alone. We feel out of control. We feel like there's something wrong with us. So we argue, trying to convince them to see what we see so we feel comfort, safety, and affirmation. This doesn't create a safe space for the other person. Instead, you're making it about you. I made things about me a lot. It doesn't matter if we were discussing tinted windows, politics, or a movie. I always pulled on that rope. And I didn't notice I was doing it so much because it had become a habit. Slowly it would put cracks in the trust with whoever I was arguing with. They would feel less and less safe to express themselves to me. This contributed to many relationships expiring.

Trying to get someone to swallow your truth will always push the other person away.

Break the cycle. If someone is arguing with you, it's probably because they're not feeling heard. So put your point aside and focus on making your partner feel heard. Once they feel heard, the argument can now turn into a discussion. Express your point. If it gets heated again, don't argue. Go back to addressing your partner's feelings, making them feel heard. Make it a nonnegotiable that you will not argue. Not just for them. For you, as a man. It takes two people to have a tug-of-war. If you refuse to hold the rope, there is no war.

You might still be asking, *Why should I back down first, especially if I believe they're wrong?* It's not about backing down. It's about choosing not to hurt people. What do you get from being right other than resentment and a stiff back from sleeping on the couch? I can't believe I'm doing this, but I'm going to quote Dr. Phil: "Do you want to be right or do you want to be happy?"

#54
Don't Inhale Your Food

I remember the daggers she shot at my thirteen-year-old friend Charlie, who was sitting right next to me with a tense face. He leaned forward toward her and mumbled through his clenched teeth, "You better not." I knew they were talking about me, the little neighborhood Korean kid they had invited for dinner that evening. But I didn't know what the big secret was. I wondered if there was something on my face.

As she bit her tongue and went back to her spaghetti, it hit me like the end of *The Sixth Sense*. Instantly I retraced all the looks thrown at me by Charlie's family during dinner. The averted eyes. The stares. The tight lips while chewing. It had nothing to do with my face. It was my mouth. I didn't close it while I was chewing.

Fortunately, family dinners, proms, weddings, business brunches, and a shitload of dates will eventually train you in proper eating etiquette if your parents didn't or you grew up in a culture where eating with your mouth open was acceptable. Of course, it comes at the expense of some social trauma. But even if you eat with your lips sealed and hold the correct fork, posture, and glass, you most likely will slip on one thing: pace.

I don't know if it's nature or nurture. I just know that when you put something in front of us, whether it's to build or consume, we go at it as fast as we can. But here's the thing: If we're focused on our food, we are not sharing the moment.

We are not expanding our communication. Instead, we are closing ourselves off. It goes back to self-awareness, but this time in an outward-facing way. We communicate by slowing down and letting someone else set the pace, by being the follower to someone else's lead. By doing this, we are joining them instead of excluding them by being in our own thoughts. We are being present. We are doing life *with* someone, instead of around. Yes, something as simple as eating at the same pace as your company is what practicing self-awareness looks like. You are aware of yourself, your actions and energy, and how they impact others. Then you make a decision to adjust so you're not making it just about you. Instead of letting your meal become a task, turn it into an experience, an exercise in stretching and growing.

Table manners.

Besides chewing with our mouth closed and eating at a reasonable pace, there are other things we can do to show the world we have manners.

1. **Open doors.** Not just for your woman or man. Hold it open for the old lady behind you. The guy in the wheelchair. The kid running in front of his parents. Or just for anyone who is coming or going around you.
2. **Treat people in service—valets, servers, bartenders, hosts—extra kindly.** Don't treat them like they are beneath you. They are making your life easier. The way you treat people in service is a direct reflection of your true character.
3. **Be present.** Give whoever you are sharing a meal with your undivided attention. Put your phone down. Genuinely want to know how they're doing and spend quality time with them.

#55
Don't Text
Like You're Seventeen

T exting is the language we speak today, especially when it comes to dating. We don't use the phone for what it was invented for: to actually call people. So instead we shoot texts and DMs to get to know someone. I get it. I do the same thing. Although I gotta say, there was this one occasion when I asked someone out via text. We never met, but we had been chatting via text for a few days. She eventually texted back, *If you're going to ask me out, I expect you to call me.* Bam. I remember pulling over and sitting there for a second thinking, *Wow, that's kind of hot.* I love that she drew a line when it comes to texting. In coaching women with their dating journey in the last ten years, I've learned that many women won't tell you how they want you to communicate with them. It's something you should already know and you will be judged on it. Well, unless you've gone through some kind of training I didn't know existed, here are the most common dos and don'ts when it comes to texting.

Do use complete sentences. Do spell words correctly. Don't overuse profanity. Do put thought into your message; have a point. Don't text just because you're bored and need someone to text you back. Don't text every two seconds. Don't get mad if she doesn't text you back in two seconds. Don't overuse emojis. Don't overuse "LOL". Do *not* sext if it isn't mutual. Do make an effort to be creative, funny, and charming. Do be considerate.

A note about dick pics.

Guys, women do not find the penis attractive. They may find you attractive and your penis is an extension of you so they choose to love it. And they may say they love your penis, but that's because it's attached to you. Your penis by itself is not hot. It never will be, no matter how big, smooth, soft, or whatever. Stop taking pictures of it. If she specifically asks for a photo of your penis, okay sure. But I bet that happens as much as you asking for a photo of her left elbow.

#56
Do Tip Well

I had a couples session once where the two fought over and over about how he tipped. She refused to go out to dinner with him because he was a poor tipper. After they would leave a restaurant, she would say she forgot something, go back in, and leave more gratuity. And she was tired of doing that. She ended up breaking up with him.

If you're the Calculator Guy, listen up: It's fair when you're with a giant party and you're the one everyone's throwing their credit cards at, but if you're out on a date or with your wife, put your calculator away. Think of what the calculator represents for her. Calculator = safe = boring. Live a little. Put the calculator away. Round up, and do it in your head.

If you're the Flashy When You Can't Really Afford It Guy, save that extra money for therapy. You will need it when you fall into a deep depression from not being able to go out anymore. When people see you tipping way more than is appropriate, they don't think you're rich and successful. They think you're annoying.

**Communicate with confidence
and generosity, and you'll
receive generosity in return.**

If you're the Ten Percent Man, another 10 percent isn't going to break you. If it is, order something cheaper or go to a place where a gratuity is not expected. The folks who wait on you get paid minimum wage and have to share their tips with busboys and dishwashers. Most are in transit in their lives. This means they have dreams. Know that your gratuity is going toward them.

One thing I hope you've taken away from this book is that the little things we do are often emblematic of larger, deeper issues or insecurities. Poor tipping is one of them. It is a moment when you are communicating with the world around you, and everyone—from the woman sitting across from you, to your boss who you've taken out to lunch, to the server who just waited on you for an hour—is giving you the opportunity to be either a boy or a man. Communicate with confidence and generosity, and you'll receive generosity in return.

EVERYTHING ELSE

This is a hodgepodge of things that will make you a man, either in every aspect of your life or in a really specific aspect of your life.

EVERYTHING ELSE, in a shot glass:

Men put thought into their gifts. Men don't chase; they attract. Men talk to children like they are people. Men don't go for the hottest girl in the room. Men aren't creepy. Men never, ever wear skinny jeans . . .

#57
Do Keep
Your Bathroom Clean

O kay, unlike making your bed or peeing in the shower, there's no bigger underlying message here. I promise. It's just a reminder, because we all forget and we also forget we will be judged on it. It's really simple. If the kitchen is the heart and the bedroom the soul, the bathroom is your armpit, and it shows your hygiene.

You better believe that she—your wife, girlfriend, or someone you just started dating—will be using all her senses when she's in your bathroom or the one you guys share. She will notice the appearance, odor, and energy. She will notice your products, colognes, lotions, your towels. The toilet—if it's clean, if the seat is up or down or loose. Anything displayed on the walls. Photos, art, knick-knacks. She will put on her detective hat, and her eyes will turn into a black light. This means she will be able to see things we don't. Like that strand of hair in the drain, the moldy shower curtain, and the slight hint of urine. She is now taking in this information and wondering if she can live with someone like this. A messy living room isn't that big a deal. But a dirty bathroom is not only a turnoff but also possibly a deal-breaker if the relationship is new. It's behavior that's telling. Little things that are big. Like opening doors, and saying, "Bless you" after she sneezes. A dirty bathroom reeks of immaturity. A clean bathroom means a clean state of mind. The "do" here doesn't mean to do it once. It means to keep it clean, always. That is where behavior is formed, patterns are broken, and growth is possible.

A dirty bathroom reeks of immaturity. A clean bathroom means a clean state of mind.

Men, here's the good news: No one expects to eat off your bathroom floor. They just want to know you're not disgusting.

#58
Don't Buy Things, Get Gifts

I have a lot of shortcomings, but one thing I really like about myself is that I'm really thoughtful in intimate relationships. I've always been this way. I care if it's your birthday or our anniversary. I care if your day was good or bad. And I want you to know that. Not to get brownie points. To give you a feeling, to make you feel loved, thought about. And one way to do that is to be thoughtful in your gifts. Maybe I had to be thoughtful because I've never had money to buy expensive gifts. But creativity pays off. I'm putting this one on the list because I've seen how much getting thoughtful gifts affects women, how much they appreciate it.

Children will gift you what they found on the way home, and it's okay because, well, they're children. Just the fact that they were thinking about you melts your heart. But when you're an adult, gifts with zero thought aren't cute. They're fast and convenient. It says you're too busy or lazy to really think about the other person and what they like. The gift is more about their giving to you in return. This is what children do. If you want to grow the fuck up, you must make it about others by putting some thought into your gifts. This doesn't mean they have to be elaborate and expensive. It just means being thoughtful, showing consideration for someone else. Proving that you know that person. And by giving them something straight from your thoughts and heart, you are giving them a piece of you.

The invention of the gift card was death to meaningful gifts. Although brilliantly obvious, it's cheating. It's like reading the CliffsNotes version instead of the entire book. Just by picking the store you want him or her to shop at doesn't turn cash into a thoughtful gift. It's not a gift. It's an easy way out. Or in. Think about all the gifts you've received in the last five years. Of the ones you can actually match faces to, which were the most memorable, and why? What's the common thread? Assuming you didn't wake up on your birthday to a helicopter on your front lawn, most likely it was the thought, the effort, and a piece of the giver. The greatest gifts always contain a part of the gifter. That is why it's memorable, unique, and one of a kind. The "holy shit" factor of a helicopter may be memorable. But a poem from your six-year-old daughter, a painting from your wife, or a handmade cigar box from your grandfather will hold more value. They move us emotionally. By putting thought into your gifts, you are sharing your humor, creativity, song, dance, words, personality, and touch. You are inserting yourself, and that is always the most valuable part of the gift.

When people say, "It's the little things," this is what they're talking about. Notes. Reminders. Messages, pieces of you, everywhere, scattered during the most unpredictable times. Not only on birthdays and anniversaries, but any day. It's not the gift; it's the thought behind it. Give when you're least expected to. That's when it will hit the hardest. Trust me: your partner will repay you in other ways. But of course, that is not the reason you are doing it. If so, you are taking and not giving.

Also, remember that a person's gift is telling of the person. This behavior defines you. It makes you an adult. It creates great stories. Putting thought into your gifts is about choosing to be selfless—sharing yourself. There's only one of you on this planet. Let the rest of us experience the rare gift that is you.

#59
Don't Overuse
Hair Product

Remember when all the male celebrities were buzzing their heads? Keanu Reeves in *Speed*. Brad Pitt in *Mr. and Mrs. Smith*. I decided to try it. Horrible mistake. I looked like a monk! I definitely couldn't pull it off. Not even close. But what was interesting was, my girlfriend at the time loved it. She wasn't just being nice. She really loved it because it was so clean. She loved running her hands over it. Everyone else gave me an "Oh, you cut your hair" comment, the *I hate it but don't want to hurt your feelings* response. Every . . . single . . . person I knew. So why was my girlfriend a fan? Because she didn't have to deal with all the shit I usually put in my hair. The silver lining of this very bad haircut was that I learned that women don't like their men to have crunchy hair. They really don't like it.

In the '50s, we used grease. The '80s, hair spray. The '90s, gel. Today, pomade? The good news is, we look less manufactured. The bad news is, we are still putting way too much stuff in our hair. Hair is important. I get it. It shapes our face and makes us feel young. But the more effort we put into molding our hair into the perfect shape, the louder we are yelling, *Look at me!* We all want people to look at us. But we don't want to announce it. It screams insecurity. The goal is to not be concerned with what others think. If we can't do that, then we must look the part. The way we do this is by appearing as natural as possible. Natural doesn't mean boring. It means pure. Honest.

We are concerned with how things look. Women are more concerned with how things feel. This means they would rather be able to run their hands through your hair than stare at it.

#60
Don't Wear Skinny Jeans

This one's personal and I stand by it. Wear pants that fit. That's all.

#61
Don't Speak to Children Like They're Children

I had a session with a young mother once. She wanted guidance through the rocky waters of "dating again". One of her biggest pet peeves/turnoffs was when she would meet someone she was really into, enough to introduce him to her six-year-old daughter, and he would talk to her like she was a child. Yes, she is technically a child, but when you speak to children as if they are children, it can come off as patronizing and approval seeking. She saw it as him trying to fit in or please her instead of just being himself. Which got me thinking . . .

When we speak to children like they're children, instead of bringing them up we are actually bringing ourselves down. Children look to us to learn, emulate, and grow. If we are acting like them, what are they learning?

Who was your favorite uncle as a kid? Why was he your favorite? Yes, there was his Trans Am, wild hair, and all the junk food he bought you without telling your parents. But it was also because he treated you like a friend, not a kid. That made you want to hang with him. He didn't talk down to you or baby you. You felt respected and important. He brought you up to his level instead of dropping down to yours. You appreciated this. He was the only one who made you feel like an adult. And now you can give this gift to children.

The way a man acts around children is a great measure of how comfortable he is with himself. Observe him around five-year-olds. Is he acting in a way he thinks he should act, or is he just being himself? Is he trying to earn points or give them? Also, watch how they act around him. Children are transparent, which means they call bullshit. They will find him either comfortable or annoying. They will either cling or cringe. And eventually, so will you.

62
Don't Go for the Hottest Girl in the Room

Here is the inner dialogue of the old me at a party: Find the hottest girl in the room and do everything you can to talk to her as fast as you can. Why? It will say you are valuable. You have worth. You're a real man.

The inner dialogue of the new me: John, look, you idiot. If the person you're attracted to happens to be "the hottest girl in the room", which is subjective, so be it. Great. But if you find yourself always pursuing the hottest girl in the room strictly because she is the hottest girl in the room, you want a trophy, not a partner. If you're looking for a badge or someone you believe will increase your worth, you are not confident with yourself, which means you cannot handle the hottest girl in the room. You will be clingy, jealous, controlling, and ultimately powerless. Remember what happened last time? Don't waste all that time and energy. Just go for who you are drawn to. Or you will always feel incomplete.

#63
Don't Be
Afraid of Women

I have coached so many men who are afraid of women. It ruins them. They end up not being themselves. Hiding. But they're actually not afraid of women. They're afraid of rejection. Here's an actual conversation with a client. Or at least how I remember it.

MALE CLIENT: Models have a waiting list. They're in high demand. Everyone wants to be with them. I can't approach models.

ME: Why not?

MALE CLIENT: I'm afraid of them.

ME: I don't think it's them you're afraid of. It's your fear of rejection, and it's fair. We struggle with society's ideas and the pressure of (A), having to be the pursuer, meaning we are expected to approach the woman; and (B), what it means if she says no. What does it mean if she says no?

MALE CLIENT: I'm not good enough. I'm a failure.

ME: Exactly. You're internalizing her disinterest as failure, one of our greatest fears. What if you didn't tie her "no" to your worth? Would that make you less afraid?

MALE CLIENT: Sure. Then it's just an opinion. Here's the catch-22. The more we fear women, the greater the chance they will reject us since fear is something that repels them. The more often we are rejected, the greater our fear will grow.

ME: Agreed. So we must break this cycle.

MALE CLIENT: But we can't fake courage. They can smell it a mile away. You have to genuinely not be afraid. This means you have to know yourself and be okay with who you are. Not something you learn in a "how to pick up women" seminar.

ME: What about this? When you see a stunning woman you are afraid to approach, besides making a conscious effort to not tie your worth to her opinions of you, know that she was once just a girl, with insecurities. Maybe also seeking approval. Know that she has a story like everyone else. My point is, look past the skin. Talk to her heart. Humanize her.

[The client ponders this.]

ME: Men objectify women when they are afraid of them. It's easier to accept rejection from an object than a real human being. If you make her human, you will be less afraid.

END SESSION

#64
Don't Be Creepy

This one's from all women in the world. They emailed me and said, "Don't beat around the bush. Make it direct."

So here goes.

Creepy is like halitosis. It comes from within. It is an energy that leaks from pores. Women can smell it like sharks smell blood. I believe this energy stems from a fear that goes way back to a lonely childhood and a lack of strong male role models. We creep because no one ever taught us healthy boundaries, how to communicate directly with eye contact and a smile. We never learned the value of courage. So we stare. We stalk. We rub against women in dark clubs, drive by the coffee shop to make sure she is with who she said she would be with. Creepy is a way of coping. A way of not facing the truth.

First, know that creepy repels people more than anything. Second, know that you can't just stop being creepy. You may be able to plug the hole temporarily, but there will eventually be another leak. Because creepy is manifested behavior arising from insecurity with oneself. In order to stop, we must explore our wiring, our fears, and begin a process of acceptance, validation, and self-love. When we truly accept ourselves, we accept others. And the act of creepy is not accepting. Simply put, to eliminate the behavior of creepy, you have to work on self. Get comfortable with you. Face your own truth.

#65
Don't Chase,
Do Attract

For most of my life I've been in a chasing state. I chased shiny things. Cars, money, women. I desperately wanted things that made me feel and look good. I cared what people thought of me. In this state, I attracted fake friends, opportunities that fell through, relationships that expired. And the less I got, the harder I chased. I lost my stance and didn't allow myself to be happy until I got what I was chasing. And since I wasn't happy, I wasn't grateful. I always saw the glass as half empty. I was negative and discouraged. So of course, nothing good happened.

After my divorce, I decided to stop chasing. I decided to focus inward instead of outward, work on me, my relationship with self, my body, my belief system. I didn't know it at the time, but I was attracting by making myself more attractive.

As I started to find my voice, courage, and passion, and stopped seeking approval and validation, good things started coming. Things that I needed to experience to learn, grow, keep building and moving toward my purpose. Money and fancy cars are not what I attracted. But that's not what I was meant to attract. I attracted opportunities that grew me as a therapist and laid the groundwork for things that would come later, like my startup and life-coaching intensive. I was attracting things that would give me tools to build a wellness platform to help others help others and my own methodology that turned into my first book.

I think that's the greatest misconception about attracting.

Attracting doesn't always mean shiny things like clothes and money, because shiny things won't take you to the next level. Attracting means getting things that line up with your purpose, that position you to head in the direction you were meant to, where you will be the brightest.

The chasing-versus-attracting state I experienced in my own life is now a concept I use with clients.

It's simple.

There are two different mind-sets we have as we maneuver through the world. We are either chasing or attracting.

Yes, both involve going after opportunities, people, dreams—everything we want and believe we deserve. And on the surface, they may appear similar. But they are very different states. And they produce very different results.

Chasing appears empowering because it is an action. You are going after something. But it is actually a depowering state. It shoots us down into a lower frequency. When we are in a chasing state, we are creating room to exchange our truth for membership. Our chasing state is lined with desperation. We tie our worth to what we're chasing, and if we don't get what we're going after, we believe we have less worth. So we give whatever or whoever we're chasing the power. By chasing we are losing our sense of self. Whenever we lose our stance—our sense of self—we are watered down and not living at our potential. Our truth. So instead of getting what we want, we become a flipped magnet. We repel.

We are either chasing or attracting.

There are two types of salesmen. The aggressive type (chaser). And the passive type (attractor). The aggressive type talks about the once-in-a-lifetime deal that you will miss out on if you don't pull the trigger. He talks over you. He doesn't see you as a person. He sees you as a bonus at the end of the month. He is desperate. He is impatient. He doesn't take no for an answer. He is in a chasing state, and all his behavior, especially his energy, is what that state produces.

Then there's the other type of salesman. This person focuses more on the connection with you instead of the product he's trying to sell. Your purchasing the product is just the by-product of that connection. He knows that the connection must be authentic and that, in order for that to happen, he must be authentic. He has to show himself by being himself. So he pulls from his Solid Self, which puts him into an attracting state. He doesn't make it about the sale. He makes it about you and your experience. He is giving instead of taking. Instead of being desperate, he is now attractive. You guys share a few laughs. You don't feel pressured. You feel safe. And you end up buying the car.

The above is a simple example of the energy and actions produced in a chasing state and in an attracting state. It doesn't apply just to salesmen. It's a life law. When we are in a chasing state, we are maneuvering at a lower potential. When we are in an attracting state, we are maneuvering at a higher potential.

Now remember, attracting doesn't mean to not be ambitious or go after what you want. It doesn't mean to sit on the couch and cross your fingers. I'm talking about a mind-set, a state, an intention, an energy, where we pull from. Not your work ethic. You should hustle and fail and learn and grind and work your fucking ass off to build what you're building. There is no other way. But not at the expense of your truth.

Attracting is a power-filled state. You are focusing on improving over wanting. You are not exchanging who you are for what you want. You are not seeking approval and validation. You are not taking. You are giving by being the best version of yourself. And sharing that unique gift. You are a prism (attracting). Not a stone (chasing). And by being in this state, having this mind-set, you are raising your vibrations, living on a higher frequency, and attracting who and what you were meant to attract.

So how do you attract? Allow me to make a motorcycle metaphor.

FIRST PISTON.

Start by listening to your truth, your authentic self. It's usually a soft whisper, because you've been ignoring it for so long. Now stand on it. That's an action. Don't just listen, but actually do or say what you feel is honest to you. Do not exchange your truth for membership. The more you do this, the easier it gets. You will get pushback. People aren't used to this side of you. You may even lose a few friends. But that's a good sign. It just means you're weeding out people who will not promote the best version of you.

This is a process. It's like a muscle that needs to be exercised daily. Listen to the soft whisper instead of your thundering voice. The latter is just your *should* voice, created by society, parents, advertising.

SECOND PISTON.

Okay, while that piston is pumping, let's talk about changing your thoughts.

Attracting isn't just about being your unique self. Our thoughts create a feeling. Depending on what those thoughts are, they're going to produce either a positive or a negative feeling—and this contributes to your state.

Out of the sixty thousand thoughts we have a day, most are . . . what? Negative. This produces a general negative blanket that covers us, and we start to get grayed out, merely existing—and I say "exist" because when you're in a chasing state, that's what you're doing. You're existing, not living. Existing is chasing. Living is attracting.

Attracting means creating new thoughts. This is a practice. You have to be aware of your thoughts and change them. Yes, it's difficult. I understand. I struggle with it every day. Because we're used to our thinking patterns. They run deep. But it gets easier the more you do it. I've come leaps and bounds from always defaulting to negative thoughts to now being able to flip the script and change them to positive ones. And the result is less anxiety, plenty of positive energy, and attracting more and better in my life, which feeds into more positive thoughts.

THIRD PISTON.

Changing your belief system. We make 95 percent of our decisions from our subconscious, from what we subconsciously believe about ourselves—and what we can and cannot do lives there. These buried beliefs were created from our story, how we were raised, when our hearts were shattered, when we were bullied—the accumulation of our experiences. Good and bad. But we always default to the bad, the doubt, the "I can't", the "I'm not good enough, smart enough, tall enough, strong enough", etc. So we must rewire. How do we do that?

New experiences. Experiences are the most convincing. We can say mantras and think differently all day, but it doesn't stick like an actual experience. It's in the experience that beliefs shift. For example, say you've never done a muscle-up. That's where you hang on Olympic rings, swing, then pull yourself up in the air and push up until the rings are at your waist. It's a common movement in CrossFit. I'm just using that example because most people can't do them. So when you witness someone doing their first one, the disbelief etched into their face is priceless. But after that one, something changes. They start to believe. They actually experienced it. And even if they can't do it again, they go into it with more confidence and belief. Eventually they can do it again. And again and again. It's no longer a big deal. The belief has been cemented. It's the same process with anything. Starting a company. Getting a woman's phone number. Building a healthy relationship. Attracting means changing your false beliefs by giving yourself new experiences.

FOURTH PISTON.

Staying in higher frequencies. This is different from just positive thoughts. These are feelings. Be love. Feel gratitude, optimism, hope, joy, creativity. You get the point. All these are higher frequencies. Lower frequencies include anger, hate, resentment, jealousy. I understand that you're human and shit happens every day. But just try to stay in the higher frequencies. Most people dip or stay at the lower frequencies. Higher frequencies = attracting. Lower frequencies = chasing.

Recap.

Focus on getting these four pistons pumping, and your life engine will move you forward in the direction you're meant to go:

1. Listening to your truth / authentic self
2. Changing your thoughts
3. Changing your belief system by giving yourself new experiences
4. Living at higher frequencies

And that will get you into an attracting state.

66
Do Hold Up

Tiny Fey once made a joke about Matt Damon and Ben Affleck being like J.Crew sweaters. They look great in the store. But then you bring one home and realize you just bought an orange sweater. Then she ends it by saying Matt Damon actually does hold up. More laughs. But as I mentioned in my own Matt Damon story earlier, he really does hold up. He's not an orange sweater that just looks good in the store. He is who he portrays himself to be. And that's what I mean by holding up.

I was definitely an orange sweater before my man journey. I wanted people to view me a certain way. What I drove mattered. What I wore mattered. Who I hung out with mattered. What *they* drove mattered. What *they* wore mattered. If Instagram was around back then, every photo on my account would be filtered. I would take photos only in fancy locations and present myself in a way that wasn't honest. There was a lot of *Do as I say, not as I do*. Basically, I was a walking hypocrite. I was flimsy. Spineless. I had no sense of self. I just wanted everyone to like me. I didn't change overnight, and I'd be lying if I told you I don't care what people think anymore. Of course I do. But I care more about my character. I try to line up my actions with my words. And I care a hell of a lot less what people think than I used to.

Do I hold up today? I don't know. It's not for me to answer. But I try to. It's extremely important to me. I think it's the greatest compliment you can give someone. You are saying they are honest with themselves. They put their money where their mouth is. They are not shaken by external forces. They are consistent, meaning safe, because that's how trust is built.

I do my best to be who I say I am. To do what I say I'm going to do. I've learned that words don't mean shit. I try to put my weight on my actions. Every time I'm not who I say I am or I sway from the character I have built (yes, character is built), I create a crack in any relationship, be it with a friend, my partner, followers on social media. And if I accumulate enough of these cracks, eventually the relationship will break. When there is a break, it's not just trust that is broken; my character is also broken. Now I'm undependable. I'm a maybe. A walking question mark.

Be a fucking period. That's what man looks like. And do that by being consistent. By holding up.

You can talk all you want, but if you don't back it up with action, you will eventually be talking to yourself.

Conclusion

Man is nothing else but what he makes of himself.

– JEAN-PAUL SARTRE

That's it. Those are the dos and don'ts that contribute to being a man. Take what you will and leave the rest. But before I conclude, I want to raise my shot glass to all the men out there who have already crossed the great divide, who are already great men. That may be you. If so, cheers. Because not everyone reading this book is where I was. There are some who may have already gone through their journey and come out the other side.

As much as we live in a fatherless nation, we also live in a world where there are great men doing amazing things every day, making huge dents in this world, and I want to acknowledge them. Because as a society, we don't. It's easy to point fingers and see shortcomings. What about all the men who are truly choosing to be a better fucking man, every . . . single . . . day?

So here's to you, the men who respond instead of react. The men who want better and decide to walk with mirrors, not in order to check their hair but rather to examine their character and be aware of how their words and actions impact others. Here's to the men who admit their defects and shortcomings and constantly strive to be better. Here's to the men who work on their relationships by working on themselves instead of trying to control or own their partner. Here's to the men who check their egos, often. Here's to the men who don't whine, complain, or make excuses. Here's to the men who wake up early and want to build something.

Here's to the men who choose to be a daily student, to learn from others instead of thinking they are better than them. Here's to the men who take care of their bodies and eat like adults, not teenagers. Here's to the men who open doors, kiss like they mean it, and love hard. Here's to the men who don't ghost. Here's to the men who return calls. Here's to the men who believe in foreplay. Here's to the men who don't live in the past. Here's to the men who have the balls to stand up to their parents and family. Here's to the men who know how to create a safe space. Here's to the men who take ownership when they've hurt someone or done something wrong. Here's to the men who believe in something greater than themselves. Here's to the men who have fire in their belly. Here's to the men who make decisions, walk with certainty, and dream big.

Here's to the men who can separate ability from worth. Here's to the men who remember birthdays and anniversaries. Here's to the men who put thought into their gifts. Here's to the men who understand the responsibility of being a father. Here's to the men who spend time and engage with their children. Here's to the men who are not afraid to show affection. Here's to the men who choose to be vulnerable. Here's to the men who say, "I love you." Here's to the men who can control their anger, alcohol, and money. Here's to the men who practice self-love. Here's to the men who are not needy or codependent. Here's to the men who stay positive through turbulence. Here's to the men who don't exchange their truth for membership. Here's to the men who understand compassion and empathy. Here's to the men who don't try to fix everything. Here's to the men who do the dishes. Here's to the men who want to make a difference.

I want to thank all the men out there who have decided

to look at themselves with courage to change; all the men making an honest effort to be good fathers, better husbands, and kinder friends; men who have sacrificed for their family, neighbors, and country. I want to thank men working in mental health, hospitals, and classrooms; men who wear uniforms—police officers, firefighters, and soldiers.

You are the true leaders of our world, and I hope to follow in your footsteps.

Acknowledgments

Harley-Davidson For giving me the feeling of complete freedom, the closest feeling to flying I have known. For my daily nectar. For connecting me with the ten-year-old in me who used to rip around the neighborhood on his little Honda Spree scooter with a shit-eating grin and without a care in the world.

CrossFit For teaching me about functional movement and reconnecting me to my body. For helping me smash my false beliefs. For pushing my body much further than I ever thought was possible.

Pharos Athletic Club For my community of friends. For excellent fitness programming and push. For my daily clubhouse, where I can just be myself, act silly, and sweat with my "boys".

My "boys" All my male friends. From the guys who were there for me while I was going through my rebirth, eating crepes in K-town and talking about our feelings, to all my boys now who I work out with, ride motorcycles with, and eat burgers with. I value all my men friends. They sharpen me and contribute significantly to who I am and who I want to be.

All the coffee shops from Studio City to Silver Lake I spent half my life in coffee shops writing my ass off. From screenplays to blogs to books. Thank you for allowing me to sit at your tables, sip your coffee, and use your Wi-Fi. Without you guys, I wouldn't have gotten anything done.

All my expired relationships For allowing me to love the best way I knew how. And for loving me back, the best way you knew how. For teaching me about love, women, and myself. For hanging in there through all the ups and downs. For scratching my back. For believing. I am sorry for the man I couldn't be.

JRNI My life-coaching and tech company. For feeding my soul. Teaching me about business and the importance of teams. Especially our CEO and one of my favorite humans, Noelle Cordeaux, who has taught me how to be a true leader, leading with vulnerability, grace, and fairness.

My Man Sheet

Below are some of the men who have influenced me in some way or another. They all have one thing in common: they are not perfect. No man is. But they have tremendous gifts and have challenged my definitions of what it means to be a man.

My father For having the balls to come to America with two little kids, a wife, and five hundred bucks. For his work ethic and humor. For loving me the best way he knows how.

My brother (Brad Kim) My parents call him "bread". And he has been that for me—a security blanket while we were growing up by taking on most of the responsibility while I went out and played. For never complaining. For being there for me, always.

My ex-wife's father For taking me in like a son. For showing me what Christmas looks like. For not being afraid to show emotions and have real conversations. For putting me on the back of his Harley with a shit-eating grin.

Bruce Lee For the simplicity in his life philosophy. He was the first man to put self-betterment into a shot glass. For creating his own martial art. For his discipline in mastering his craft. For coming to America and marrying out of his race when that was frowned upon.

Wayne Dyer For his everyman approach to spirituality. For teaching me, on my little nightly walks, about love and how our thoughts will determine everything. For demonstrating the power of a gentle spirit.

Jack Kornfield For bringing Buddhism to the West and talking about it in plain English. For his teachings about inner strength, kindness, and compassion.

Bruce Springsteen For living at the intersection between masculinity and vulnerability. For representing the everyman, the American Dream, a shot at the title, a possibility, a chance, for being a T-shirt-and-jeans guy.

Charles Bukowski For his raw, brutal honesty. You may love or hate him, but there's nothing more honest than a Bukowski poem.

Quentin Tarantino For flipping the script: breaking the rules with long pages of dialogue and nonlinear storytelling, which we were taught not to do in screenwriting class. Standing up for his art as well as to Hollywood.

Matt Damon For holding up. For the way he handles celebrity and fame. For sitting with me when I was running a club and treating me like I went to high school with him. He's also a pretty good damn actor.

John Gottman For all his life's work on marriage and relationships. Showing us the red flags and how important creating a safe space is. And the importance of the six-second kiss.

The Rock For his work ethic. For his motivation, humility, charisma. Every time I wake up at 5 a.m. to work, I joke about being the "Korean Rock" (as I think about him and how he does things daily).

Tony Robbins For being the first life coach. For reminding us of the importance of our physical state. For feeding over 100 million people through his "Feeding America" charity that stems from him growing up poor and giving back after someone fed his family one Thanksgiving.

Chris Spealler For his athletic ability and humility. For proving that David can beat Goliath. For hanging a poster I made in his CrossFit box without knowing me. For coming to Los Angeles and doing a video course with me. For his faith and dedication to his family. For being just an all-around good man.

Sylvester Stallone For his incredible true life story behind Rocky. Broke AF and eating sardines yet still holding his ground to star in a movie he wrote. For his determination. For his belief in himself. For buying his dog back.

Henry Rollins For being the everyman, coming down with us instead of at us, ridiculous work ethic, and his wealth of knowledge. For being unassuming and humble. For his honesty and channeling anger for positivity instead of destruction.

Gary Vaynerchuk For his "document over produce" approach to content and giving value instead of trying to sell something. For his no-excuses attitude and stance on being a good person and liking humans.

To all my guy friends (too many to list) For crepes and conversations in Koreatown while I was going through my divorce. For pushing me with my fitness. Burger nights. Chats about guy stuff and women and dating. For riding motorcycles with me. For accepting me and allowing me to act stupid and be myself. For reminding me how important it is to have male friends in my life. You are all good men.

Recommended Reading

The Way of the Superior Man: A Spiritual Guide to Mastering the Challenges of Women, Work, and Sexual Desire, by David Deida

Fire in the Belly: On Being a Man, by Sam Keen

The Obstacle Is the Way: The Timeless Art of Turning Trials into Triumph, by Ryan Holiday

Facing Codependence: What It Is, Where It Comes from, How It Sabotages Our Lives, by Pia Mellody, with Andrea Wells Miller and J. Keith Miller

Mindset: The New Psychology of Success, by Carol S. Dweck

Recommended Listening

"Simple Man" by Lynyrd Skynyrd
Reminds me to be a simple man. I've listened to this song hundreds of times while riding my motorcycle.

"The Man Comes Around" by Johnny Cash
The song I listened to for hours while walking the streets of San Francisco as I was thinking about a title for this book. It gave me certainty and hope for man's return.

"Born to Run" by Bruce Springsteen
Reminds me of America and the '80s. Freedom. Working hard. Building things. Opportunities. Engines, convertibles, and wind. Everything I love.

"Lose Yourself" by Eminem
The song that gets me the most pumped when I CrossFit or want to push myself harder than I think I can.

"Wishing Well" by Airborne Toxic Event
Reminds me of my rebirth. First motorcycle. First tattoos. Had this song on replay as I hugged canyons and zipped to the beach on a Ducati. It made me feel alive.

"Runaway" by Kayne West
I love how honest he is in this song about all his defects and weaknesses with women. I listened to this often as I reflected on my own.

"Oregon" by Tez Cadey
I've listened to this song a hundred times, on walks and while lying on my living-room floor visualizing all my dreams and everything I want to build.

"Change" by Tracy Chapman
I cried uncontrollably to this song when I was going through my divorce and knew I needed to change. Played it many times for the teenagers I was treating in rehab.

"Ultra Violet (Light My Way)" by U2
Lots of listens to this song on night walks by myself. It always made me feel close to God. It gives me light. Makes me feel like I can walk through trees.

Brené Brown's TED Talk "The Power of Vulnerability"
The best TED Talk ever. She opened the door on vulnerability and proved that it makes you strong, not weak.

About John Kim

John Kim (The Angry Therapist), LMFT, pioneered the online life-coaching movement seven years ago, after going through a divorce that led to his total rebirth. He quickly built a devoted following of tens of thousands of fans who loved the frank and authentic insights that he freely shared on social media. He pulled the curtain back and showed himself by practicing transparency and sharing his story—something therapists are taught not to do. Kim became known as an unconventional therapist who worked out of the box by seeing clients at coffee shops, on hikes, in a CrossFit box. He built a coaching team of his own and launched a sister company called JRNI, creating a new way to help people help people and change the way we change.

You can meet him at
www.theangrytherapist.com
IG: theangrytherapist
Facebook: www.facebook.com/theangrytherapist
Medium: www.medium.com/@angrytherapist
JRNI: www.jrni.co